CW00793223

AIMING FOR AN A IN CfE HIGHER ENGLISH

Support for Students and Teachers

DICK LYNAS

New Generation Publishing

Contents

Acknowledgements

To the *Scottish Qualifications Authority (SQA)* for kind permission to refer to Specimen CfE Higher English questions and to refer to official specifications for CfE Higher English as available at www.sqa.org.uk. The *SQA* is not responsible for any content omissions or inaccuracies in this Guide; nor does permission to refer to any of the specimen questions or specifications imply that the Guide is an essential form of support, or the only suitable form of support, for CfE Higher English candidates

'Assisi' and *'Sounds of the Day'* from *'The Poems of Norman MacCaig'* by Norman MacCaig are reproduced by kind permission of Polygon, an imprint of Birlinn Ltd (www.birlinn.co.uk)

'Glasgow Sonnets 1' from the collection, *'Collected Poems'* by Edwin Morgan is reproduced by kind permission of Carcanet Press Ltd (www.carcanet.co.uk)

Thanks to Ms Elaine Millar and students at Our Lady's High School, Motherwell, for commenting on early drafts and to Mr Jim McNeill for advice on design.

Thanks to friends and family members who allowed their answers to questions to be used as examples

Any oversights with regard to copyright will be acknowledged in future editions

*Dedicated to aspiring CfE Higher English
students everywhere*

About the author

Dick Lynas is a former Principal Teacher of English and examination marker who went on to become a secondary school head teacher before setting up a consultancy in school leadership and management. He is registered with *Education Scotland* as a Career-Long Professional Learning (CLPL) provider

Throughout a long career in education, Dick also tutored family members and friends who were looking for support with their preparations to sit Higher English exams. His Guide comprises the advice for each of the three parts of the Higher English exam that two generations of students seem to have found most helpful. It also includes examples of answers that he or they have provided in order to illustrate the written outcomes of that advice.

The material has been updated to take account of the new format of the CfE Higher English course and exam that is introduced in Scotland from August, 2014.

Dick's other books include:
Developing Excellent Team Leaders: A peer-coaching approach for teachers who aspire to middle or senior management posts in schools (Authorhouse, 2011)
Pies Were for Thursdays: An autobiography (Authorhouse, 2010)

x

About the book
Introduction

Search through online student chat rooms after any Higher English written exam over the years and you will discover that as many as 40% of the students' own comments are of the 'could-have-done-better' variety. So why didn't the students in question do better?

Scotland's Curriculum for Excellence (CfE) aims to provide a coherent, flexible and enriched curriculum for 3-18 year olds. The CfE Higher English course and written exam, to be introduced in and after August, 2014, reflects these three overarching principles. The new exam format, in particular, assesses your ability consistently to *demonstrate in writing* to the person who will mark your paper three fundamental abilities:

*   Your ability to *understand* the *content* and structure of your own written work and the written work of others
*   Your ability to *analyse* your own literary *techniques* and the *techniques* of others for *putting over* content
*   Your ability to *evaluate* the extent to which you and others have succeeded in putting over content *effectively*.

Unfortunately, given the limited amount of available time, a written examination can only ever test a small sample of the skills in question. So a possible answer to the question above is that the candidates who could have done better had not provided their best samples of these three key abilities on exam day. Simples!

It is a little like having all the knowledge, skills and commitment that you need to fill a post for which you have applied - and then not getting the job because you failed to communicate those attributes fully enough on the day to the interview panel. Fortunately, there is a series of *strategic, tactical* and *operational learning skills* that you can develop through practice as you prepare for the exam in order to maximise your chances of doing well on the day.

Strategic learning skills are concerned with your overall longer term *planning* on how to *gain* knowledge and then *demonstrate* it by means of your writing skills under examination conditions; tactical skills are concerned with the way you *prioritise* your use of study time for examinations; operational skills are concerned with making best use of the *time* available on the examination day to write your best possible answers.

This brief Guide explains how to make the best use of these learning skills to improve your *answer-writing* abilities. Using specimen questions, it also provides examples, all drawn from personal sources, of what can be achieved in answers, even under exam conditions. We begin with an overview of the new CfE Higher English Course before turning to a more detailed analysis of each paper.

Overview of the CfE Higher English Course and the Exam

A CfE Higher English Course is designed to cover two units of work that, taken together, promote coherent development of the key skills of reading, writing, listening and speaking at a suitable level of complexity.

Unit 1: Analysis and evaluation: this unit promotes and assesses the reading and writing skills that you need in order to be able to *demonstrate* your ability *to* understand, analyse, evaluate, summarise and compare texts of a reasonable level of difficulty from English literature, language and the media; speaking and listening skills are also developed, demonstrated and assessed through practice in speaking about and listening to discussions about such texts.

The word 'demonstrate' is highlighted here because the single greatest failing among otherwise competent and capable candidates is the failure to demonstrate fully under exam conditions, especially on exam day itself, the skills that they have. And unfortunately, the external marker who assesses those skills only has your answer papers to go on.

Unit 2: Creation and production: this unit develops the skills of writing and speaking and in particular those that you need so that you can demonstrate your ability to create and produce detailed and complex language in both written and oral forms; listening and reading skills are promoted through practice in reading and hearing about how others use these skills.

Typically, as a candidate, you are covering a course of study that meets the demands of the two units by reading, discussing and writing about examples of drama, poetry and prose, including, possibly, filmed or televised productions of English literature. You will also have been studying, discussing and writing about newspaper and magazine articles that deal with a range of current issues.

Level of skills
How good do your reading, writing, speaking and listening skills need to be if you are aiming for an A in CfE Higher English? It is hard to specify levels exactly although we shall be looking at *marking criteria* and *category descriptors* later. As a broad guide, you should be able to read, understand, write about and replicate articles of the standard that is to be found in 'quality' newspapers. We return to this point later.

You should also be able to write concisely, coherently and yet comprehensively about a range of works of literature in the time available in the exam. The examples of folio pieces, answers and critical essays that are provided in this Guide will give you a good idea of the standard that is looked for if you hope to do well.

If you have understood clearly the points that have been made so far, then you can take it that your reading skills are well up to the mark. All you have to do then is demonstrate them under exam conditions - and that is where your ability to write relevantly, concisely yet comprehensively comes into play.

Internal and External Assessment

The CfE Higher English examination combines *internal* assessment and *external* assessment *of* the two units. Internal assessments of the four skills of speaking, listening, reading and writing are conducted by your own teachers, using agreed criteria for that purpose to ensure consistency. This Guide focuses on the *external* assessment of the units, where your *written* work is assessed by an external marker who does not know you. This marker is the *audience* for whom you are writing.

It is essential for you to keep this simple fact in mind as you work your way through the various externally assessed sections of the exam. Candidates sometimes do less well than they might have done in exams because they forget who their audience is and neglect to write what they think is obvious.

Just remember that the person who will be marking your papers knows nothing about your answer-writing skills until you have *demonstrated* them as fully as possible in an answer book. There's that word again! Do not be surprised if it is repeated a few more times.

We turn to a summary of the three parts of this Guide and the three papers by which the two units of study are externally assessed:

Part 1: The Writing Portfolio
Part 2: Understanding, Analysis, Evaluation
Part 3: Critical Reading.

Then we look at the demands of each paper in detail and at a range of sample answers of the quality you should aspire to if you are aiming for an A.

Part 1: The Writing Portfolio
The *Writing Portfolio* is the major way in which you *demonstrate* the quality of your own extended written work. It comprises two examples of your work, one that is broadly *creative* and the other which is broadly *discursive*. Each piece of writing is assigned a mark out of 15 with final marks totalled to provide 30 marks and hence 30% of the final total. The portfolio is submitted on a due date ahead of the final exam.

Part 2: Understanding Analysis Evaluation
Understanding, analysis and evaluation (UAE) samples your ability to *understand*, *analyse* and *evaluate* two passages of previously

unseen prose. A series of questions test your detailed understanding of, and your ability to comment on:

- the *content* of passages (*what* the writers are saying)
- the *style* of the passages (*how* the writers put content across)
- the *effectiveness* of the passages (how *well* the writers put the content across)

More precisely, you are being tested on your ability to *demonstrate* in *writing* your understanding and appreciation of these aspects of written English.

Think of the difference between knowing how you feel about someone or something and being able to put those feelings so clearly into words that other people will understand perfectly well how you feel. Being able to communicate what you know and how you feel with such precision that a third party can say I know what you mean and I know how you feel is a high-level skill. That is the kind of precision that your answers need.

A total of 30 marks are available for this section of the exam, a further 30% towards the total. You have *1 hour and thirty minutes* on exam day to get them.

Part 3: Critical Reading
From August 2014, *Critical Reading* comprises two sections. One section requires

you to *demonstrate in writing,* by answering a series of questions, your *understanding, analysis* and *evaluation* of a single extract from a set Scottish text (drama, poetry or prose) before then inviting you to comment on similar or contrasting features between the specific extract and the writer's other work. This section of the *Critical Reading* paper is rather like answering the questions on the two passages in the *UAE* paper, although in this case you will have seen the material before.

In the other section, you are required to compose a critical essay that *demonstrates* your *understanding, analysis* and *evaluation* of any other piece of literature of your choice so long as it is from a different genre from the section 1 extract. A total of 40 marks for the paper, 20 for each section, brings your overall potential score to 100%. You have *1 hour 30 minutes* on exam day to impress your marker with your analytical reading, critical evaluation and composition skills.

We turn now to a detailed analysis of each of the three papers that comprise the final written exam and provide examples of what can be achieved in the time available ahead of and also during the exam with regard to planning, prioritising and producing excellent answers to questions.

Dick Lynas, September, 2014

Part 1: The Writing Portfolio

a) Introduction

The writing portfolio is your opportunity to impress your marker with your ability to compose written pieces of your own, as opposed to your ability to *understand, analyse* and *evaluate* the work of others. You are invited to submit, ahead of the final exam day, two written pieces of not more than *1300* words each, one that is broadly *creative* and one that is broadly *discursive*. Previously accounting for 20% of the marks in the exam, the folio accounts after August, 2014, for a whopping 30%. So you certainly want to get in among these marks from an early date.

A creative essay involves you in writing as clearly as possible either about an important event in your life or about an imaginary situation; a discursive essay requires you to explore the pros and cons of a given current issue or to provide your own point of view about a current issue in such a way that you succeed in persuading your reader at least to consider your point of view.

b) Timing

This is the one part of the exam where time is not really an issue. You will have all the time you want to draft and re-draft your two pieces before submitting them ahead of the final exam day. There really is no excuse for not doing very well in this part of the exam, assuming that you have the necessary literary and literacy skills in the first place. All you have to is satisfy the criteria!

c) Criteria

Criteria are statements of the standard of performance that has to be achieved in some activity for a given award to be made. In athletics, for example, runners usually have to achieve a certain time in their event before they can be picked for the national team.

Similarly, national criteria are specified with regard to the quality of answer that you should produce in the various parts of the CfE Higher English exam in order to score a given number of marks. And it is the marks that you score, compared with the marks that everyone else sitting the same exam scores, that will decide if your final grade is **A, B, C** or **D**.

You will not be surprised to discover that the priorities identified in the next section of this Guide are: to make yourself aware of what the various criteria are for each part of the exam; then to study very closely the *Category Descriptors* that describe what a high-scoring performance should achieve in each part of the exam; and finally to look at examples of very good answers in each paper so that you will know what they look like.

In this connection, note that the *Scottish Qualifications Authority (SQA)* issue each year after the event the criteria for each of the three parts of the exam – the *Writing Portfolio*, the *UAE* paper and the *Critical Reading* paper

- together with detailed marking instructions for markers. Study closely criteria and marking instructions from the past as the *principles* underlying them will also apply in your year.

Your writing in the portfolio is assessed, in essence, in terms of its *content, structure* and *expression*. Markers are advised that top marks can only be allocated to writing in which:

- Content is very well-selected and demonstrates the qualities of clear insight, imagination and sophisticated thought
- Structure is well-organised and enhances the overall impact of the writing
- Expression demonstrates good word choice, good use of literary techniques and well-constructed sentences

d) Meeting the criteria
Part 1d (i): Planning

Planning your portfolio comprises two basic stages (a) gathering material and then (b) composing a final draft of your work. Gathering material will depend upon whether you are working on your creative essay or your discursive essay.

Gathering and jotting for a personal essay

Your personal essay is likely to take one of three forms - a *narrative* essay, a *descriptive* essay or a *reflective* essay.

Narrative essay

A narrative essay tells a story. It details a sequence of events and focuses on how the people or creatures involved in these events behave

Descriptive essay

A descriptive essay focuses on describing one or more scenes. There may be no action but the outcome is a word-picture of the scenes being described

Reflective essay

A reflective essay focuses on a series of thoughts or ideas that the writer shares with the reader. Again, there may be no action but the outcome is an insight into the ideas and emotions of the person sharing them. A Shakespearian soliloquy is a reflective essay.

A possible solution

It is quite difficult to sustain a purely descriptive or reflective essay for 1300 words so it might be an idea to write a narrative essay that not only tells the story of a sequence of events but which includes elements of description of people and places and reflection by you about the significance of the series of events. And if the events really happened then your personal account is likely to be that bit more powerful.

When you are jotting down the events in question and assessing their impact on you, it is a good idea to remember that information and feelings come to us through our five senses – sight, hearing, smell, touch and taste. So jot down the things you saw, heard, smelled and tasted. Describe also how you felt physically and emotionally. The sequence in which events unfolded will provide you with a basic structure for your essay, although you may wish to try your hand at flashback or flash forward.

Direct speech can make your writing livelier so jot down the things that people said and the way in which they said them. Your vocabulary should be suitably mature so spend a bit of time as you draft and redraft your notes, asking yourself if your choice of words is as effective as it could be (See much more on *word choice* later)

It is also perfectly acceptable to use slang or colloquial phrases as you seek to convey an authentic picture of the way in which people spoke or behaved. If, however, everyone you met was 'really nice' and everything that happened to you was 'really amazing' then you can be really confident that your word choice is really poor.

Literary techniques
In your various jottings, make use of literary techniques such as *word choice, imagery, sentence structure* and *tone* that professional poets, dramatists and novelists use and which you will no doubt have learned about as part

of your studies for the *Critical Reading* section of the exam (about which, more later)

Imagine, if you like, that you are composing the kind of biographical or autobiographical literary piece that could be the subject of an appreciative critical essay by a candidate in a future exam. Your aim is to convey the nature of your experiences and your reflections upon them with such *clarity* and *sincerity* that your marker can identify with them and empathise with you. George Orwell's essay, '*A Hanging*', which is the subject of a critical analysis later, is an excellent example of the kind of creative writing you should aspire to use.

Researching for discursive essays

Researching for discursive essays involves most of the above again. This time, however, you can expect also to be involved in a fair amount of fact-finding about your chosen topic. As with the *personal reflective* option above, it is likely that you will produce your best work if you seek to write a *persuasive* essay on some topic that matters greatly to you and about which you have some strong views.

You may well be willing to acknowledge that other people have other views on the matter in question but your main focus will be on putting your own case as strongly as possible, with objective evidence to back you up. Statements which are biased and prejudiced and lacking in any evidence in support of their validity will not impress your marker.

On the contrary, securing a top grade will certainly require a carefully structured and linked sequence of points that conveys reason and conviction. Use the simple kind of layout that is provided with the advice on *structure* that is provided later in this section.

Courtesy of the internet, modern exam candidates are a click of a mouse or a tap and swipe away from literally millions of sources of information on their chosen topic. Sourcing and researching topics of all kinds has never been easier. Make good use of the facility but do not forget to note and acknowledge any sources that you may use. A good persuasive essay will resemble the kind of passage that is used in the *UAE* part of the exam.

Part 1d (ii): Prioritising Criteria

First make sure you familiarise yourself with the official *SQA Candidate Guide* for the CfE Higher English Folio and with the *Category Descriptors* for folio work that you can find along with the marking instructions for specimen papers. Focus on producing a *Category 1* performance in each of your two pieces. Other perfectly normal candidates have managed this, so why not you?

Choice of topic

No apologies for repeating that the next and perhaps the most important step you take will be to choose appropriate specific topics for your two folio pieces. If you are aiming for an A, it is absolutely essential that you should choose topics that really do matter to you. It is also vital that the topics in question should be serious and complex enough to enable you to write at some length on them. Exploring your preference for chocolate over vanilla ice cream might not be demanding enough.

Topics that matter

Given that candidates tend to produce their best writing when they are writing about something that they know and care a lot about, it is suggested that your *creative* piece should be an autobiographical narrative of some important personal event in your life that you have reflected upon and learned something from – unless perhaps you already have a well-developed talent for fiction writing.

Similarly, the best sample of your *discursive* writing is likely to be when you are trying to persuade your reader about the importance of some issue that really matters to you rather than exploring in a rather academic way the pros and cons of an argument or writing a report on a topic that does not interest you.

Too personal

Candidates sometimes shy away from writing too personally but it is worth remembering that your writing will not be made public and markers are bound by a strict code of confidentiality. If, however, you do not want to be too personally revealing then your next best step, so far as a creative essay is concerned, is to write a short story about something important that happened to someone else, basing your story firmly on an experience of your own.

That way, you will be able to draw directly on your own memories of and reflections upon a significant event while attributing them to an imaginary persona. Most great writers base their stories in personal experience anyway so you will not be alone if you decide to write about imaginary events that nevertheless reflect your own life and interests.

Suitability

Spend some time thinking about suitable topics for each type of essay. With regard to a personal essay, hopefully you have never had a really distressing or momentous experience but there is bound to have been some sort of learning situation in your life that had an impact upon the way that you think about things. The event might even have been trivial so far as other people were concerned but if it mattered to you and if you can communicate to your marker just how much it mattered then you will score highly.

With regard to a discursive essay, just think. Is there any issue where you would be delighted to persuade others to agree with your point of view? Perhaps you have enjoyed studying and debating an issue in your social subjects, science or RME classes. Perhaps you enjoyed a TV debate or documentary on some issue. Perhaps you would like to share your passion for a hobby. Perhaps there is a type of person whom you admire, or detest. These are the kind of topics to choose. The examiner is inviting you to get on to your soap box and let rip so go ahead and do so - making sure that you avoid racist, sexist or otherwise offensive language.

We look later at some examples of the kind of writing that can be produced by writers who really care about the issues that they are discussing.

Writing: Purpose, audience, point of view and structure

While you are puzzling over which topics to choose, you should be taking conscious note in your reading of the many ways in which professional writers compose their work. The CfE Higher English written exam tests your ability to *understand* and *analyse* and *evaluate* the work of others. But it also tests your ability to *synthesise, or compose,* clear and coherent *extended* written work *of your own* for your portfolio. You may find the following discussion useful for composing your own work for the folio and for writing the critical essays that are discussed in **Part 3** of this Guide.

Reasons for writing

Writers are consciously or subconsciously aware of two fundamental aspects of their writing – its *audience* and its *purpose*. Who are they writing for, and why? The answers to those two questions determine the genre or type of writing they produce, the contents and style of that writing and the stance or point of view that they adopt.

We may state with some confidence that most writing is produced because the writer wants to inform us, entertain us, share an experience with us or express a point of view about some topic; and the very fact that the writer makes his or her writing public suggests that he or she is keen to persuade readers of the value of the information, the experience or the view-point that is being shared. Naturally, therefore, writers will use a range of techniques that help to express the 'message' of their work in as powerful and memorable a way possible.

One of the major questions in the *UAE* paper deals precisely with how a writer's point of view influences what the writer says and the way in which he or she says it. We return to that topic later when we discuss evaluation questions in **Part 2** of the Guide.

In the meantime, jot down as you work through any articles that you read the answers to six recurring questions:

- What is this about?
- Why has this been written?
- Who is it for?
- What are the consequences for content and style?
- What is the writer's opinion?
- How do I know?

Structure

Structure is concerned with the way we place words in a sequence to build sentences; the way we place sentences together in a sequence to make up paragraphs; and the way we put paragraphs in a sequence to create extended writing.

We shall be looking at the structure of individual sentences later when we discuss language features in **Part 2** of the Guide (although it might enlighten you to *deconstruct* the previous sentence right now) Meanwhile, given our focus here on the extended writing that is required for the portfolio, we shall examine how such extended writing is structured.

Persuasive Essays

We look first at the structure of a typical *persuasive* essay. This is because it is a good idea to write such an essay as one part of your portfolio submission and also because both passages in the *UAE* paper typically take the form of persuasive essays.

When modern writers compose a persuasive essay, they tend to follow a simple, underlying sequence of parts:

- a beginning, in which the writer announces what the essay is going to be about
- a middle, in which the author develops and exemplifies the points that he or she is making.
- an end in which the writer sums up what he or she wanted to say.

Modern writers use fairly short paragraphs, comprising usually five or six lines of writing with a short space between each group of lines. Each paragraph in its turn will typically comprise three – five sentences, which, taken together, present the points which contribute to the overall 'message' of the essay.

The sentences usually comprise:

- an 'opening', 'lead' or 'topic' sentence which says what the paragraph is about
- two or three other sentences which develop, exemplify and explain the point being made
- a concluding sentence that sums up a point before moving to the next one.

Thereafter the writer is likely to follow a similar pattern, paragraph by paragraph – a topic sentence presenting a main point followed by examples and explanations of the point – until eventually the writer has completed the points that he or she wishes to make. Very often the writer will end with a paragraph that sums up his or her overall 'message' for a final time, sometimes repeating key points as a means of so doing.

It is worth noting at this point that a persuasive essay of the length that you will have the option of writing for the portfolio and analysing in the *UAE* paper will make only around half a dozen *key* points. The rest of the essay will comprise one or more *examples* of points or *repetition* of points (we come back to this when we discuss *summarising* skills)

Sometimes, for the sake of making an impact, the writer may begin a paragraph by asking a question to catch the attention of the reader before then going on to provide the answer(s) to the question. On other occasions, again in order to catch the attention of a reader, the writer may begin, especially in the case of the opening paragraphs of an article, with a dramatic specific example or illustration of the point that he or she intends to make later in the paragraph before then going on to make the general point. Occasionally, the writer might devote a whole paragraph to examples of a point or a little anecdote that exemplifies the point before or after making the point.

Distinguishing between a *point* and an *example* of a point is a key skill in reading any piece of work. Practice improves that skill. Typically, the language that a writer uses to express a key point is more generalised, more complex and more difficult to understand than the language that is used to provide examples of a point.

Within each paragraph, link words or repeated words will connect each sentence to the next one so that there is a logical flow of ideas throughout a paragraph for the reader to follow. Link words and repeated words also help to connect one paragraph to another so that the reader can follow the flow of the writer's overall 'message' from paragraph to paragraph. Each article is like a chain of information and each paragraph is a link in the chain.

A sequence of links between the sections in a persuasive essay might look something like the following:

In recent times there has been a great deal of debate about; Some people say that; But I believe that; This is because; Furthermore, it seems to me that; Then again, I also think that; I would also like to point out that; It is also true that; I am sure that; Yet; Nevertheless; Clearly, therefore; This means that; in conclusion, I strongly believe that...

Occasionally there may be a short paragraph to indicate a summary, linking or turning point.

Go back over the passage that you have just read and try to identify *five* key points that the passage makes about structure and *three* different ways (with examples) of how links are made (a) within sentences (b) between sentences and (c) between *paragraphs.*

Part 1d (iii): Answering questions

By answering questions, we of course mean in this case submitting to the Exam Board the final drafts of the two essays that you have written for your portfolio, one broadly creative and the other broadly discursive. What might these essays look like?

Number crunching

Let us begin with some number crunching. You are allowed to use up to *1300 words* for each essay, *but no more.* Shall we agree that your best chance of achieving an A in each piece is to write an essay of such breadth and depth of content that you will need most if not all the words allowed, rather than the *650* that are the minimum allowed? Good – although we do understand that quantity alone is not enough.

As a ballpark figure, we may estimate that each sentence that you write will consist of around 20 – 25 words. If we assume that each paragraph will comprise 4 or 5 sentences then it looks as if each paragraph will add up to around 80 – 125 words. So you are looking to compose around 12-16 paragraphs in each of your essays, with each paragraph suitably linked coherently to the next one. You should end up with two essays that have a logical flow of ideas, while keeping within the required word limits. So beware of non-sequiturs.

Sophistication of language
There is, of course, the small matter of the sophistication of language with which you express thoughts and feelings in your essays as well as the clarity of their structure. Appropriate *word choice*, striking *imagery*, varied *sentence structure* and an appropriate *tone* will all contribute to the quality of your written work. We explore these language features in detail in **Part 2** of the Guide but be aware that the advice given there about *analysing* and evaluating the writing of others is every bit as relevant here as you compose your own writing.

Examples
It is time to look at a couple of essays that were made earlier. The creative essay that follows combines a mixture of narrative, descriptions and reflections. It is based on the candidate's interest in immigration procedures last century in the USA.

In the persuasive essay, the candidate made use of his extensive study and love of music to present his case. Unusually, there are no source references in the second essay for the simple reason that the writer's views are all his own. Both offerings are examples of what can be achieved when someone is really interested in a topic and drafts and re-drafts his or her efforts to communicate that interest to markers as clearly as possible.

Example of a personal/reflective essay
Isolation in the Metropolis

This city will kill me. The grime, the corruption, the insincerity, the concrete - all will rise and place a knife in my back, smirk and then twist. The air isn't pure. Every second I stay here, more filth will invade my lungs. My innocent boyish looks have gone. I stare into a mirror and the cold, hard features of a stranger return my gaze. The pain seared into my eyes speaks to me most clearly of all about the damage that the Big Apple has caused me.

I remember that, as the boat approached the city, the green icon of freedom loomed over us. Oh, the joy I felt! This euphoria seemed to ripple through my fellow passengers; weeks on this floating prison had expelled the hope of an American Dream for many, but Lady Liberty seemed to reignite a flame in us all. We were herded off the boat and led onto nearby Ellis Island.

I had heard of the trials of this place, where the Americans seemed to sort the fit from the disabled. On the boat, I had secured friendship from a Polish family. They were the type of people who took in the sick, cared for the weak, and swore by their faith. I had become fascinated with them, their unabashed optimism shone throughout the boat. They had brought along their disabled grandmother with them, a woman bound to a chair, every tragedy that had ever befallen her etched into the deep wrinkles of her face and reflected in her weary eyes.

The family, in contrast, were beacons of health. The mother was affectionate and charming, the father exuded stoicism and masculinity, and the children, ripe with energy, sowing joy into the torn faces of the other passengers. They painted the picture of an idyllic immigrant family, and would have looked at home on a leaflet about the American Dream.

When I stepped onto the Island, the dream was shattered. Guards ushered in the broken and beaten travellers to the hall for processing. Stripped of our humanity and clothes, doctors analysed us one by one, picking those who seemed fit enough to meet the "American Standard".

An inspector came to me, his small eyes analysing my whole person. The man seemed to suit the situation; his features sharp and clinical, a large nose like a beak, pecking inquisitively at the new arrivals, sorting the people of value from the liabilities. With a piece of chalk, he placed a tick on my vest and ordered me to proceed to the next station.

Behind me on the line, the Polish family were inspected. The mother flashed a smile at the inspector, and told her children not to worry. One by one, the family were processed, all of them deemed fit for America, until the inspector rested his eyes upon the frail grandmother. With no hesitation, the doctor chalked an ironic cross on the woman, and ordered a guard to wheel her back to the boat.

Astounded, I asked the family if they were going to go back with her, thinking that such kind, noble people would sacrifice their shot at capitalism for a beloved family member. The answer was a resounding "no". The mother's permanent smile broke, trembling. In hindsight, I realised that the corrupting air of New York had already got to them, their supposed values and principles undermined by the Dream.

But was I any different? My mother had pleaded with me not to go. I would surely find work sooner or later on a farm, she assured me. It would break her heart if she were never again to see her beloved son. But I had been adamant. I was not willing to live the life of toil and poverty that had been my father's lot. A new world beckoned and I wanted to make my fortune...

A year has passed since then, and within those twelve months I have become jaded and torn. The city has broken me. New York is lit by the saturated lights of capitalism, but I have never been in a place so dark. For the past hour, I have sat in my cell of an apartment, conjuring up my memories and trying to pinpoint where it all went wrong. I am surrounded by millions of people, yet I have never felt so alone.

The dilapidated state of the apartment reflects my time in New York; I have little by means of possessions, my cupboards harbour no food, and the walls smell of damp and foul rot. I spend my time here filling my room with the sound of my coughing and listening to the bustle of the city. I did not smoke until I came to New York. Now, it is one of my few pleasures, a narcotic escape from the misery.

The streets are awash with crime; thugs battle each other for the area and prey on the weak. The police are just institutionalised thugs; they glower in the streets, and display vulgar abuses of power, trying to shake order back into the community. The Americans preach the good word of their Founding Fathers and declare that America is the most civilised place in the world. I see no democracy here, no social mobility. This America would be alien to Benjamin Franklin.

I get dressed, don my coat and brave the Atlantic winds. As I step out of the door, I become another hopeful trying to make it in New York. All the broken faces I pass reflect my own crisis. I enter into the fray of the city, tall building close in on me, blocking out any natural light. Shops dazzle with their displays, beckoning me, seducing me to take part in this grand masquerade of consumerism. The people of this town like to believe that objects will reconcile their disenchantment with the city, but they know that no jewellery or suit will cure their insatiability. I peer down an alley, and see a man being mugged. I fix my head straight on, and carry on walking. Being a Samaritan would be too dangerous.

Truly, New York is about the survival of the fittest. Only the most vicious, narcissistic predators float to the top. Human compassion has perished. I find sanctuary in my mind; memories of a lost future ricochet in my head, my past ignorance warming my soul. I have lost everybody and everything, I came to this country not seeking riches, but just seeking a life. The American Dream is a cruel joke, with my fate as the punch-line.

Sample persuasive essay
Is All Music Art?

In my honest opinion, I would say that music is the best form of entertainment. It speaks to us in a way that other forms of media such as television and cinema cannot. My view is that this is because music invites us to conjure up pictures and moods in our imagination. Pictures help us to appreciate what something or someone looks like or feels like. But music allows our imagination to run free. It has been the theme of revolutions, the sound of change and the hymn of tragedy. But, is all music art?

Well to answer this question, we must ask another: "What is art?" The definition of art is a personal thing. Many would say that art is anything created by man, others would say that art is only found in cold silent galleries adorned with paintings. In my humble 16 year old opinion, the definition of art is something created by humans which conveys emotion. But then, what about music? Does every single song released contain emotion?

There is a whole spectrum of genres, each offering something different. It could even be said that certain genres revolve around one particular emotion. For example, pop music revolves around love, punk music revolves around angst and rap music revolves around insecurities about how much money the rapper makes.

Even genres such as dance or electro-ambient revolve around emotion. Dance music, indeed, is very much concerned with emotion and the dance movements themselves are often a bodily expression of the emotions that one feels. All genres of music are concerned with the expression of emotion in different ways.

Everybody has a favourite song. Personally, my own is "Walk on the Wild Side" by Lou Reed, as it paints the picture of the hazy, reckless youth that Reed revelled in. But everyone has a different taste in music. As I said before, musical types have a different emotion closely connected to them. I found, through asking some of my classmates what their favourite song is, that most of the music an individual listens to reflects their personality. Yes, you could call it stereotyping, but I like to call it 'educated guessing'.

Optimists nod their heads to the beat of pop, cynics dwell on the "old classics" trying to capture the glamour and essence of the baby boomers sonic revolutions. Or to put it more kindly, quieter, more introverted folk in the class seem to like one type of music whereas the more extrovert characters seem to like music that is a bit more expansive.

Sometimes, the lyricist can be incredibly personal, speaking from the bottom of their soul about their own failings or feelings. For example, the Joy Division album "Closer", penned by Ian Curtis before he tragically took his own life, narrates the inner-monologue and torment that plagued Ian in his final days. He articulates himself beautifully in his lyrics, particularly in the song "Heart and soul", which seems to describe the woes of his own personal life, such as the affair that shattered his marriage: "existence well, what does it matter? I exist on the best terms I can, the past is now part of my future, and the present is well out of hand".

Music also affects the world in ways other art forms cannot. For example, music acted like a cannon, firing shells of psychedelia that caused the explosion of colour that is 60's flower-power, the drug- induced roars of bands like The Grateful Dead, assaulting the minds of the blossoming liberal youth. This caused American pop-culture to evolve, transforming what was once a conservative grey segregated country into a land of colour, free thinkers and mixed-culture.

In our own country, music indicated how the society was feeling; the rebellion and anger of the punk movement highlighted the alienation the youths during the trend of rich glam-rock and consumerism, the mod subculture tapping their smart shoes to the beat of Small Faces and The Who at a time of repair and stability in the UK. In the 80's, the abrasive and harsh electronic sound of Kraftwerk infected the public, reflecting the environment of concrete and brutalist architecture.

Electronic dance was popularised in the 90's and has been a big musical genre since. It has changed dramatically, from Adamski's 'Killer' to more progressive forms such as Daft Punk's "Derezzed". But, can we call these almost robot-like and manufactured beats art? What emotion do they convey? I believe that even electronic melodies made on a Macbook are, in fact, art. Dance music conveys an emotion of unity, happiness and euphoria. Like it or not, Disclosure's "White Noise" can be called art, and is not lesser art then Bach's 'Toccatta and Fugue in D minor'. You could even see electronic artists as modern day composers, constructing complicated symphonies, not using violins and cellos, but synthesizers and laptops.

Now here is one issue. Can Nicki Minaj's 'Starships' be on par with a masterpiece such as Beethoven's 'Moonlight Sonata'? Sadly, yes. As much as I hate the canned and uninspired music of Miss Minaj, it still can be considered art. The song still conveys an emotion of recklessness and euphoria. Yes, the emotions may be simple and shallow, but then again, I suppose so are her audience's emotions. They are all 7 years old, by the way. However, the grooves of Abba and Beyonce all have a cross-generational appeal, taking people back to their own youth, labouring over tape compilations of The Bee Gees making their cassette player debut.

Instrumental music can also be emotional. There may not be lyrics to preach them, but the style and musicality conveys it. In fact, often times just the melody can convey a deeper emotion that words just cannot. For example, if the music is slow and sombre, in a minor scale, then it is probably a melancholy, depressing track, while if the song is upbeat and in a major key, then it's probably a positive song.

The instrumental album "Young Team" by post-rock outfit Mogwai seems to lift us to another world, and this is achieved by a large, open soundscape. Music cannot only deliver emotion, but it can also inform and narrate. The Velvet Underground's debut painted the picture of the outcasts and hedonists found in the darker crevices of New York.

In conclusion, I believe that all music is art. To me, music is a very special thing indeed. Sometimes music can even shape whole life styles and perceptions, just like religion. Music is art and there is nothing better than a warming melody to have most people hooked.

The Smiths' even saved somebody's life with their music. (1100 words approx)

Assess the two portfolio pieces that you have just read, using the *SQA's* marking criteria and category descriptors to do so.

(NB: The two portfolio pieces have been typed in line with SQA advice but this Guide is published on A5 rather than A4 paper - so do not be too demoralised about the apparent length of folio pieces and sample critical essays!)

Part 2: Understanding, analysis and evaluation (UAE)

a) Introduction

There are some significant changes to *UAE* part of the CfE Higher English paper from August, 2014. For one thing, the total number of marks available drops from 50 to 30, a mere 30% of the total available instead of a previous 40%, good news for those who have traditionally struggled with this part of the exam.

You will be presented with two passages of unseen prose that deal with a *common* topic but detailed questions will be confined to the *first passage* only.

There will also be a single *comparison* question that invites you to identify similarities or differences between the ideas and points of view of the writers of both passages. You will very quickly grasp that, overall, the paper assesses some very familiar abilities.

Thus questions on the first passage assess your *ability to explain:*

- the *contents* of the passage (*what* the passage is about)
- the *style* of the passage (*how* the writer puts points across)
- the *effectiveness* of the passage (how *well* the writer succeeds in achieving his or her purposes)

Your *understanding* of *contents* is also assessed by the *comparison* question which requires you to identify, via the language of the passages, and to *summarise, in your own words,* key ideas in *both* passages that are either similar to or different from each other.

b) Timing

You have *one hour and thirty minutes* to answer questions adding up to 30 marks. This is a very generous time allocation, not least given the fact that, in the past, one hour and 45 minutes was allocated to securing 50 marks.

Simple arithmetic tells you that you can devote three minutes to achieving each mark. On the evidence of the specimen *UAE* paper issued by the SQA (more of which later) the time that you spend on an individual question is likely to range from around six minutes to around fifteen minutes. You might want to spend a little longer in making sure that you score all 5 marks for the comparison question (see a sample answer later)

Timing tip 1

Although there is something to be said for skim-reading over the first passage before answering any questions, a glance over the specimen paper issued by *SQA* (see below) suggests that you do not need to do so.

In their kindness, the examiners provide a brief summary *in italics* of what the passage is about (so do read it!) and then they indicate clearly in their questions the lines in the passage where you are likely to find the answers to the questions, starting at the beginning and working your way steadily through the passage. It is almost as if you are being invited to answer one or two questions each on six or seven mini passages (note, however, that the type of question is no longer indicated by **U, A or E** - more on this later)

The following approach to answering questions on the two passages is suggested:

(i) Begin by reading the *comparison question* at the end of passage 2 (but not the actual *passage*) to find out if it is inviting you to identify the ways in which the two writers *agree* or *disagree* over key ideas.

(ii) Then go directly to question 1 on the first passage, after reading the examiner's summary of the passage, and then focus on those lines in the passage that are referred to.

(iii) Answer the question as best you can but **as well as doing so,** jot down in a *brief* phrase, aside from the answer, what you think the *key* point is in the section of the passage that you are dealing with and *underline* for later reference any key word or words that you think convey that key point.

(iv) Proceed in the same way through the first passage, answering question after question, *briefly* jotting key points on the side as you go for later evaluation. If a question asks you how one part of the passage links with what has just been said or what is just about to be said, you will, of course, need to read both parts of the passage.

By using this approach to answering questions, you will be preparing to do well in the *comparison question* (probably the most difficult question of them all) as well as answering the *current* question. Furthermore, if you think about it, you will realise that the questions being asked are a good clue to those parts of the first passage that the examiner feels are most important and which are therefore likely to feature when you are later invited to *compare* or *contrast* key points between the two passages.

Timing tip 2
It is essential that you try to answer all questions so do not dwell over a question for so long that you simply never reach the questions at the end (that includes dwelling too long on jotting down key points and underlining key phrases as you answer questions) That is how to penalise yourself twice if, in the event, the answer that you eventually give to the difficult question is wrong! Enter the number of any question that you are not sure of in your answer booklet but then proceed directly to the next question.

That way, you will make sure that you give yourself the time to try all questions. You can then go back to unanswered questions, by which time you will have understood the passage better, and so may have a better go at answering any questions that were giving you problems first time around.

Timing tip 3

You will be pleased to know that the quality of your extended composition skills are *not* being tested in this part of the exam but rather your ability to focus on specific words, phrases or sentences and to explain their meaning or impact in as *clear* a way as possible.

So settle for providing one or more *phrases* or *bullet points* as answers, depending on the number of marks available rather than long-drawn out time-consuming answers. For example, there is no need to repeat the words of a question in your answer. In the case of the comparison question you could even draw up a little list of numbered points, together with evidence from both passages that indicate shared or opposing views. Or you might introduce lists of points with a colon and separate individual points with semi-colons

Timing tip 4

Although analysis and evaluation questions focus on analysing and explaining the contents, structure and style of English prose, there is no requirement to learn in great detail the technical language of *grammar*, the study of how words, sentences and paragraphs are constructed. Many a candidate has done very well in Higher English without knowing the difference between *gerund* and *gerundive*, *caesura* and *enjambment, synecdoche* and *metonymy* for example.

Yet some command of the technical language of grammar will allow you to answer many questions on the content and style of a passage much more *quickly* and *clearly* than explaining a technique in a roundabout sort of way. So it is well worth learning some grammar. We return to this point later when we look at sample answers.

c) Criteria
If you are aiming for an A in the *UAE* paper, you will need to be able to demonstrate in *writing in the time available* the following skills:

- Your ability to demonstrate, *in a concise yet comprehensive way*, your *understanding* of key points or items of information, examples of points and links between points
- Your ability to *analyse in a clear and thorough way* the writer's use of *words, imagery, structure, punctuation and tone* to emphasise the points being made
- Your ability to *evaluate* the effectiveness of the passages in a way that shows that you *fully appreciate the purposes and point of view of the writers* and that you can use critical terminology *accurately* and provide *supporting evidence*
- Your ability *to summarise key ideas and to identify similar or contrasting points of view* of two writers dealing with the same topic.

d) Meeting the criteria
Part 2d (i): Planning
It is nonsense to think that there is nothing that you can do to plan how to handle the demands of questions on previously unseen passages of prose. The following advice will increase your chances of scoring well in this part of the examination, whatever your current levels of literacy are.

Past papers and specimen papers
First, get hold of as many *past papers* and *specimen papers* as possible and set yourself a timetable to work your way through the questions that are set in the *UAE* sections of those papers, making sure that you tackle and answer questions within the *time* limits allowed.

Study the marking instructions and sample answers that accompany each past paper as these make clear to markers (and therefore to you!) what is being looked for. *Study in particular the SQA CfE Higher English Specimen Paper that exemplifies the kind of passages and questions that you will face after August, 2014 (on which, more later)*

You will also find very useful, the SQA guidance about types of questions in past papers that are still relevant for the new format of this part of the exam (see the final entry in the *Selected sources of further advice* pages of this guide)

In past years, teachers used to volunteer to be markers, not because they wanted to become millionaires but because they wanted to learn about what was being looked for so that they could pass on tips to their students.

Nowadays that kind of information is freely available to every student via the papers and marking instructions that are published annually after the exams by the *SQA*. It would be quite unforgivable if you were to disregard that indispensable form of support. Details about the availability of past papers going back ten years and more (with the more recent ones easily accessed via the SQA web site) are listed in the *Selected sources for further study* pages of this Guide.

It would be desirable if you tackled, under exam conditions, one past paper per month in the August-May run-up to the external exam. Alternatively, complete one past paper per week in the last month or so ahead of the exam, noting any similarities in the pattern of questions that have been asked in the past.

The examples of questions and answers that are provided in this section of the Guide are intended to illustrate the points that are made about demonstrating in writing your ability to *understand*, *analyse, evaluate* and *summarise* as fully and yet as succinctly as possible in the time available the points the writers are making.

They are, however, no substitute for the real thing. If trying out past papers and specimen papers and then analysing marking instructions does not improve your ability to demonstrate in writing your *understanding*, *analysis* and *evaluation* of prose passages then you should probably abandon your studies in English.

Other reading
A skim reading of these past papers makes it clear that the prose passages that are presented in this part of the examination always deal with current *political, economic, social or technological* topics (think PEST!) Recent topics have included, for example, the carnage of World War 1, the impact of shopping malls on consumers, drugs in sport and the effects of video games on levels of literacy.

So if you have not already done so, it is high time that you started reading articles in quality national newspapers and their weekend magazines (online or in paper copy) that deal with such topics. Examples that come to mind include, in alphabetical order, weekday and weekend editions of the *Guardian*, the *Independent*, the *Mail on Sunday*, the *Observer* and the *Times*. Many local newspapers also offer articles on these kinds of topics – the *Herald*, the *Press and Journal* and the *Scotsman,* for example. Many articles on relevant topics are also available on the internet. Google a topic and you will find millions of articles!

Part 2d (ii): Prioritising

Read again the earlier article on the structure of persuasive essays and, as you work your way through the kind of persuasive essays that have been typically used in past papers, see if you can identify examples of the points that were made in that article.

The more often you do this, the more effective you will become at recognising recurring features of English prose and the more fully you will understand the passages that are presented for your consideration.

Part 2d (iii): Answering questions

Given the criteria that were listed earlier, you can expect questions that will involve you in exploring:

- *Lexis-* the meaning of *individual words* and *phrases*
- *Syntax-* the way words and phrases are structured into English *sentences*
- *Link words-words that create connections between sentences*
- *Word choice and how it is used to put over a point*
- *Imagery and how it is used to put over a point*
- *Sentence structure and how it is used, with punctuation, to emphasise points*
- *Tone and the ways in which it reflects a writer's point of view and key ideas with regard to a topic*

Types of question
As the title of this part of the exam indicates, there are three types of questions on the first of the two passages:

- Questions that test your *understanding* of *what* the writer is saying - the *content* of the passage
- Questions that test your ability to identify and *analyse* the techniques that the writer uses to put points across - the *style* of the passage
- Questions that invite you to *evaluate how effectively* the writer has used a technique - the quality of the passage

Being extremely kind and thoughtful people, the examiners use verbs such as *identify*, *explain* or *show* how, *analyse* or *evaluate* in their questions to indicate the type of question being asked and the ability being assessed. And if there are two parts to a question, the examiners make that clear as well. The examiners may no longer use the **U, A, E** code to help you to identify the type of question being asked but you will never miss it so long as you read questions carefully.

As if all of that was not enough, the examiners also provide you with a major clue about the number of different points they are looking for by indicating the number of marks that are available for each question.

As a rule of thumb, assume that one mark is allocated to each relevant point that you make up to (but not more than!) the total available for each question. Half of the 30 marks are allocated to questions on *content* (including the 5-mark comparison question) and the other 15 marks are allocated to questions on *style.*

As a final act of kindness, the examiners, as noted earlier, indicate clearly the lines of the passage where you will find the answers to the questions being asked, allowing you to work through the passage from beginning to end.

Questions that test your *understanding*

Such questions relate to issues of *lexis, syntax* and *link words* as described earlier.

They typically take one of three forms:
- **Content questions**
- **Context questions**
- **Connection questions**

Content questions ask you to identify and explain *in your own words* one or more of the points that the writer is making about the topic of the passage. Imagine that you are translating a foreign language into English except that here you are 'translating' English words into their simpler English equivalents. Answer with one specific point per mark awarded. You will receive no marks if you simply repeat the words of the passage, even although you might have correctly identified the word, phrase or sentence that provides the answer.

Candidates sometimes complain that they used the words of the passage because as far as they were concerned the meaning was perfectly obvious and needed no explanation. Unfortunately, the only time that the examiner can be sure that you have understood the contents of a passage is when you use your own words to explain the points being made. The examiner knows nothing about your literary and literacy skills until you *demonstrate* them!

You will not, however, receive marks for providing more correct answers than is indicated by the number of marks being awarded. Do not waste time by providing four or five different answers to a question that offers only one or two marks. It is not a bad idea, however, to provide where possible, one more point from the passage in your answer than the marks awarded, just in case one of your points is wrong.

It is not, however, a clever idea to answer questions from your general knowledge rather than from the information that is in the passage. You are like members of a jury who are required to come to a verdict on the basis of the evidence presented in court and not on what they heard in a bus queue.

Context questions invite you to *identify* a nearby word or phrase that helps to clarify the meaning of a given word or phrase. Simply quote and justify your choice unless you are asked to do more than that.

Connection questions relate to the various ways in which writers connect one point to another, one sentence to another and one paragraph to another in order to provide a coherent flow of ideas in their writing. In English, links are made as follows:

• the use of *conjunctions* (joining words) such as *and, so, therefore, accordingly* to indicate an *ongoing flow* in the specific points being made

• the use of *conjunctions* such as *but, however, despite this, yet, on the contrary* to indicate some *switch* in the flow of the specific points being made

• the repeating of *words* from one sentence to another to emphasise connections between the specific points being made

• the use of *demonstrative pronouns* (more grammar!) such as *this, that, these* or *those* to refer to a specific point that has already been made

• the use of *adverbs* like 'obviously', 'naturally', 'certainly', 'indeed' to suggest that something is true when it is only a point of view

• the use if the word 'even' to suggest that there is something surprising or extreme about the point that is just about to be made.

Quote one or more examples of these types of linking techniques in your answer and then explain precisely how they indicate an *ongoing* flow or *change* in the flow of the specific points being made.

Given the nature of questions on the understanding of words, you may find the following useful:

Lexis or the meaning of words and phrases

Your grasp of vocabulary will ultimately depend upon the amount and quality of reading that you have undertaken throughout your life and the trouble that you have taken to find out what words mean.

There are one or two tips, however, for you to practise that can help to maximise your understanding of words in the exam when you are not sure of their meaning.

(i) Synonyms

We noted in the section on the structure of prose passages that, for the sake of clarity and emphasis, writers in English very often repeat points. When they do this, they often use *synonyms* (words that mean much the same as the words that they used to make the point first time around)

This being the case, there are many times when you can figure out what a word means, even if you do not know its meaning, by checking other words nearby that you do understand. Sometimes, indeed, questions invite you to identify words that help you to understand the meaning of other words (see samples later)

(ii) The source and structure of words

Your grasp of vocabulary will be assisted if you have studied Latin or Greek or a modern foreign language. Many English words come from these other languages and if you happen to know the meaning of the foreign word then you can work out the meaning of the English equivalent. You might be able to figure out, for example, that a *facile* argument is one that is just too easy or simplistic if you happen to know that the same word means *easy* in French. Similarly, you could figure out that a *neologism* is a new word (from Greek *neo* meaning new and *logos* meaning word) Then again, it might be all Greek to you.

All is not lost, however, if you have not studied such languages. More difficult words are often quite long and comprise *a prefix, a stem and a suffix*. Look, for example, at the word, *incomprehensible*. The word can be broken up into its prefix (*in*), its stem (*comprehens*) and its suffix (*ible*) So long as you have an idea of the meaning of *comprehens* (think, for example, of friendly locals on your holidays who ask you *comprende?*) and with a little bit of logical and lateral thinking you might work out that the word means *not able to be understood*. Such 'sideways' thinking may help you to get at the meaning of a word by looking for connections between its use in the passage that you are reading and uses in other contexts that you can think of.

Parsing or classifying words

There are ten *parts of speech* (nouns, verbs etc) or *word classes,* as they are called nowadays, into which every word in the English language can be fitted. You should develop the skill to be able to explain into which part of speech/word class a given word falls and then explain its use (adjectives are describing words, for example) Candidates who familiarise themselves with these ten parts of speech/word classes will be better able to comment on an unusual use of a part of speech.

For example, an old grammatical rule says that you should not begin a new sentence with a conjunction (and, but, so etc) because conjunctions are by definition words that join two separate sentences or statements together into one sentence.

Similarly, logic suggests that you should not end a sentence with a preposition because a preposition is a word that is positioned in front of another word. Writers will, however, often break these rules precisely in order to draw the reader's attention to some point they wish to emphasise. Knowing the rules means knowing when they are broken – and why Given that lexis and syntax are aspects of grammar, you may find that the following short introduction to grammar is also useful:

Grammar
There was a time when pupils spent many hours studying *grammar*, the rules by which English words are composed, used and linked together to make sense. Grammar has a language of its own and so pupils learned how to *parse, analyse* and *synthesise;* they could explain the uses of a *noun,* a *pronoun* and an *adjective*, a *verb*, an *adverb* and a *participle*, a *conjunction*, a *preposition* and an *interjection*; they could even explain the difference in use between the *definite* and the *indefinite article.*

They knew the rules of *syntax* and the differences between the four *forms* and the four types of English *sentence*; they knew their *principal clauses* and their *subordinate clauses*, their *adjectival clauses* and their *adverbial clauses of time, place and condition*; they knew all about the *tense*, *voice* and *mood* of verbs; they knew how the *punctuation* of a sentence helps the reader to make sense of what is being said; they could name and explain any *figure of speech* and they knew the difference between *rhythm, rhyme and assonance*; the difference between *a homonym and a synonym; and even the difference between a gerund and a gerundive.*

Alas, no more!

A wide range of books on the basics of English grammar is available and a very useful recent example is listed in the *further sources* pages. Dipping into such books from time to time to check on some grammatical point is highly recommended for any candidate who would like to score well in the examination This is because the basic structure of the English language has changed little over the years and having an understanding and a command of the technical language of grammar sharpens your ability to explain *briefly and succinctly* how a writer uses (or disobeys) various grammatical rules to compose prose and put points across.

Sample questions and answers to questions on our understanding of content, context and connecting words

What follows is a short passage that exemplifies the use of content, context and connecting words. There is no substitute for the real thing, however. Download as many past papers as you can access from the SQA and other web sites, together with their marking instructions. They are an indispensable aid to understanding the requirements of the close reading paper. They also provide vital information concerning what your marker will be looking for in your answers. If you are wondering at this moment if you have already seen this advice, then that is because you have. Judicious repetition is at the very heart of teaching!

The detailed questions and answers that follow are constructed for the purpose of exemplifying and clarifying the points that are being made in this section of the guide, rather than replicating the wording of questions that appear in exams.

The Specimen CfE Higher English paper that was mentioned earlier does that most effectively and we shall be discussing that paper later. The short passage which follows explores the reasons why so many of us enjoy films that feature comic book heroes.

'It is no coincidence that the films that we watch these days frequently deal with the impossible. The adventures of comic book characters such as Superman, Batman, Iron Man and Spider Man, together with the recurring efforts of the likes of Bruce Willis to die hard, are served up in apparently endless sequels. **These** largely computer-generated adventures do little to explore the deeper aspects of people's characters as they cope with real-life encounters. It is enough that good versus evil and good always wins – for a while at least until the next follow-up when the bad guy returns to cause more mayhem, before once again being consigned to eternal, or at least temporary, damnation for the disturbance he has delivered. **Yet,** adults and children swarm to watch them. Why do they attract such numbers?

It must surely be a form of escapism. The economic crisis of recent years, together with the endless news of international tensions and climatic disasters make for gloomy viewing and reading. It is wise to escape from our financial worries and woes in particular every now and again and watching the miraculous feats of the mighty can be an inexpensive solution. There is, however, another reason why we are attracted to such apparently childish adventures. It is because we never quite lose the child that is in us. **And** we all share a secret dream that perhaps for us one day the impossible will become the possible'.

Example 1-understanding and answering content questions

'It must surely be a form of escapism' Identify three types of worry from which we might be trying to escape. (3 marks)

Sample answer (a)

Three types of worries that we are trying to escape from are the economic crisis, international tensions and climatic disasters.

This answer provides three correct examples of worries. But there is no effort on the part of the candidate to use his or her own words. Therefore the examiner does not know whether or not the candidate actually understands the meaning of the phrases in question and the answer deserves a score of *0 out of 3*. The marker won't even take pity on you and award a half mark for at least recognising the correct examples.

Past candidates have admitted that they knew the meaning of words and phrases such as 'economic crisis' but had assumed that the meaning was obvious and did not require explanation. Assume that the marker knows nothing. Bad tactics all round! No marks and time wasted!

Sample answer (b)
We worry about not having enough money to live on.

This answer is short and to the point and in your own words but it only scores 1 mark out of 3 as only one example is given. Why settle for 33%?

Sample answer (c)
We worry about:
  (i)   not having enough money to live on
  (ii)   the possibility of war between different countries
  (iii) severe weather

This answer scores 3 out of 3. Three different sources of worry are provided in the candidate's own words. The answers are expressed briefly but very specifically in three 'bullet points' that save valuable time. Good tactics all round!

If, however, you are finding difficulty in explaining any particular concept in your own words then put down the appropriate answer number, leave a blank space and go back at the end. Tip No 1 about not spending too much time puzzling over difficult questions is relevant here.

Example 2-Understanding and answering context questions

Example 2(a): Explain how two other words from paragraph 1 help the reader to understand the meaning of the word 'recurring' and how one word from paragraph 2 helps the reader to understand the word 'mayhem'.

Sample answer: 'sequel' and 'follow-up' help us to understand that 'recurring' means happening again and again and 'disturbance' helps us to understand that 'mayhem' means some kind of upset (this answer is not only correct but as before it is brief and to the point)

Example 2(b): Explain how the phrase 'real-life' might help a reader to understand the phrase 'computer-generated'

Sample answer: the phrases are opposite in meaning; real-life' tells me that the way real human beings behave is not the same as the impossible way in which they behave in situations that have been created by a computer programme.

Example 3: Understanding and answering connecting word questions

Sample question: In the passage about comic book films, what use is the writer making of the three underlined words, These, Yet and And?

Sample answer: The word 'These' helps the writer to provide a flow between the point he was making about these films in the previous sentence and the new point that he is about to make about the films in the current sentence, moving from comic characters to real people.

The word 'Yet' helps to emphasise the point that despite the fact that the films are quite shallow, as explained in the previous sentence, nevertheless, and perhaps surprisingly, people love them, as is pointed out in this new sentence.

The use of the word 'And' indicates to me that the writer is going to add a point that relates closely to and possibly even repeats the point he has just made about childhood and not growing up. As a conjunction, 'And' is not usually used to begin a sentence so the fact that the writer uses it in this way suggests that he wants to attract our attention to the importance of his final point about our hopes for the future.

Questions that test your ability to *identify* and *analyse* techniques

Typical *analysis questions* usually ask you not only to *identify* some literary or language technique that the writer is using to put over his or her 'message' but also to *analyse* or explain *how* the technique works.

Remember, you are *not* being asked here to 'translate' the writer's words into your own words as if answering a question on *understanding*. So an answer that explains what words *mean* rather than analysing their effect will score no marks. (We return to the notion of *meaning* and *suggestion* later when we discuss the *denotation* and the *connotation* of words)

Passages in the *UAE* part of the English exam are almost always of the *persuasive* variety that we discussed earlier. There are four major literary/language techniques that essay writers use to express and persuade us about their point of view:

- **Word choice**
- **Imagery, or figures of speech**
- **Sentence structure and punctuation**
- **Tone or mood**

Analytical questions will focus on one or more of these techniques so read each question carefully. If, for example, you are invited to comment on how the writer uses *word choice* or *imagery* to emphasise a point, you will receive no marks for explaining how the sentence is *structured* or *punctuated* –

even if what you say is correct! The same applies the other way round, of course. Sometimes you may be asked to comment on two or more of these techniques and in such cases it will be essential for you to provide *one* example of each of *two or more* different techniques.

The four literary techniques
Word choice
As you will no doubt have learned from your study of English literature in general, and poetry in particular, words and phrases may be used for their *denotation* or their *connotation*. *Denotation* is the literal meaning of words as defined in a dictionary whereas *connotation* is concerned with the various associations that words may set off in our minds.

Word choice, like imagery (see below) is usually concerned with the *connotation* of words rather than their *denotation*. The writers of the kind of prose passages that you can expect to come across in the Higher English *UAE* paper try all the time to choose words that convey as clearly and persuasively as possible the points and opinions that they are trying to put across to their readers.

Scored out words in original manuscripts of poems, plays and novels often provide evidence of the writer's desire to find just the right word to convey a point and quite often there are fine distinctions in meaning between an original word or expression and the final version. So you can expect questions that invite you to identify and explain the effect on the reader that certain specific words have.

To take a simple example of the distinction between denotation and connotation, words like *stroll, stride, saunter* and *march* are all basically concerned with walking but they convey pictures of folk walking in quite different ways and in different moods. *She marched up her neighbour's driveway to complain about the noisy children* provides a very different picture from *she strolled up the driveway to chat to her neighbour about the holidays.*

The writer could have used the word *walked* in each of these examples but I hope that you can see that the fine distinctions in meaning and connotation that are conveyed by *marched* and *strolled* make them better word choices in terms of trying to get a clear picture across to the reader of the brisk and determined way in which the first person was going to do 'battle' with her neighbour compared to the leisurely relaxed way in which the second person was going for a friendly chat. This matter of writers trying to express themselves in as clear and interesting way as possible through their careful choice of words is at the heart of every question about word choice - not to mention your own writing.

Imagery

Imagery is linked to the connotation of words as it is concerned with the use of words in a way that goes beyond their literal meaning to set up *mental pictures* or *associations* that relate to one or other of our senses - sight, hearing, smell, touch or taste.

If, for example, a student speaks of going through *an ocean of reading* while preparing for an exam, we understand that the writer is not speaking of a literal ocean but simply creating in our minds the image or picture of a vast expanse of water to emphasise just how much reading the student did.

If a writer speaks of '*crunching* through the snow *crystals* before *crossing* over the *crackling* ice', we appreciate that the writer is trying not just to describe but to *imitate* the sound of someone walking through the snow to cross over a frozen lake. We can almost *hear* the sound being made (especially if we read the words out loud) as the person walks along thanks to the deep and hard sound of the individual italicised words and the repetition of the hard '*cr*' sound.

You will have learned from your study of poetry in particular that when words are used in a way that goes beyond their literal meaning they are called *figures of speech*. Most commonly, such figures of speech relate to our sight or our hearing. The two most common figures of speech that relate to our sight are *simile* and *metaphor* and the two most common figures of speech that relate to our hearing are *alliteration* and *onomatopoeia,* a technique that is much easier to remember than it is to spell!

Simile
As the name suggests, the writer using a simile is identifying one way in which two different concepts are similar. Similes always use the words 'like' or 'as' so they are very easy to identify. The purpose behind their use is always to provide the reader with a kind of mental picture of something that helps the reader to understand more clearly the point being made. Take the simple example, *he fought like a lion.* We know that people are not really like lions but the writer is using the simile to emphasise the strength and ferocity with which the man fought.

Metaphor
When a writer speaks of one concept as if it *really was* another quite different concept and not just *like it* then the writer is using *metaphor.* Metaphors are by far the commonest figures of speech in the English language. Indeed, we often speak of *metaphorical* language when we really mean *figurative language* (It's a little like using the word *hoover* when we really mean *vacuum cleaner* or *biro* when we really mean *ballpoint pen*) Like similes, metaphors are used to give us a mental picture that will help the writer to

emphasise in an interesting, more memorable and clearer way the point that he or she is trying to make by implying that it is some other quite different thing.

When Shakespeare describes Macbeth as 'Bellona's bridegroom' or 'valour's minion', he is emphasising Macbeth's fierce bravery by describing him as if he is the husband of the goddess of war or a servant of bravery itself. (Admittedly the metaphor does not work very well if you do not know who Bellona is or what 'valour' or 'minion' means!) When Hamlet wonders whether it is better to 'suffer the slings and arrows of outrageous fortune or to take arms against a sea of troubles', Shakespeare is emphasising the many times that we have problems in our lives and what we can do about them; he describes fate as if it was an enemy firing arrows at us while we have to decide whether to fight back like soldiers or give in to problems that are so extensive that they seem like the sea. I am sure you will agree that Shakespeare's way of putting it is much more picturesque than mine.

The metaphors in the prose passages used in this section of the English exam are usually quite striking as writers seek fresh and unusual ways of saying something. Sometimes, however, writers fall into the trap of using metaphors which, although they might once have been fresh, are now so overused that they have become *clichés*. There was a time when the word *amazing* meant something; now through overuse, like the word *nice,* it means practically nothing. Writers occasionally use clichés deliberately in a kind of mocking way.

Alliteration and onomatopoeia

These are the figures of speech that provide written English with a soundtrack (if you will forgive the metaphor) In the case of alliteration, a writer uses a series of words all beginning with the same letter to imitate the sounds of the scene that he or she is describing. Letters such as 'l', 'm' 'n' 'p' and 's' convey a soft and gentle sound whereas letters such as the hard form of 'c' 'd' 'g' or 'k' provide a hard and harsh sound. Quite often, however, a writer will use alliteration mainly to catch the reader's eye in order to bring to his or her attention a particularly important point that he or she wishes to make, often in the form of a metaphor. (Notice the title of this Guide, for example)

Onomatopoeia is the use of individual words that have been created to imitate a sound – *'tinkle' 'crash'*, *'bang'*, *'boom'*, for example. Or think of the *cuckoo,* so named because the word imitates its peculiar *whistle* (itself another example of onomatopoeia) You might be interested to know that a *kittiwake* is another example of a bird that is named after the sound it makes, but perhaps not. At their best, the use of such words can even help to win Eurovision Song contests (Think of Lulu singing *Boom Bang-a-bang* all those years ago with appropriate musical accompaniment to convey the racing of her heart when her loved one was near – try *You Tube* if you are too young to remember)

Other figures of speech

Other figures of speech that feature from time to time in the passages in the close reading paper include *personification, hyperbole, rhetorical question, paronomasia (or pun for short)and oxymoron.*

Personification is a type of metaphor where a creature or an inanimate object is spoken of as if it is human. As with all figures of speech, it is used by writers to emphasise their points in a striking, clearer and more memorable way. Hyperbole is the use of exaggeration to emphasise a point, often in an amusing way. Rhetorical questions do not really need an answer. They are asked simply as a means of drawing the reader's attention in a more focused way to the points that the writer wishes to make. *Pun* (or paronomasia as it is known for long as opposed to short) is a play on the meaning of words to emphasise points in a witty way. Oxymoron links words of opposite meaning together to emphasise that a person or situation can comprise a mixture of totally contrasting qualities. Thus, in the case of Romeo and Juliet, parting is such sweet sorrow.

We do not have the space here to work through every figure of speech with examples but it is certainly worth your while to find out all about them because an ability to recognise, explain and use them will certainly improve your literary and literacy skills.

Sentence structure and punctuation
There's that word *structure* again. The vast majority of sentences in English, including this one, consist of statements. Some, however, take the form of *questions,* (including *rhetorical questions*) or *commands* or *exclamations*. Do not therefore be surprised if you are asked to comment upon sentences of a less common form. Answers to questions about sentence structure should never be about *word choice* or *imagery* or *tone* but rather should be about the very *order* in which words are placed. Watch out for:
- especially short or especially long sentences
- questions, commands or exclamations rather than statements
- sentences with no verb
- sentences that switch the subject with the object
- sentences that begin with a conjunction or end with a preposition

The order of words in a sentence is always about emphasising points in the sentence. Quite often an unusual form of sentence will accompany a particularly striking image so that the writer is doubly emphasising his or her point. A longer sentence, for example, often makes a list of points building up to a climax (or sometimes an anti-climax). This is a way of placing great emphasis on the last point in the sequence.

Other sentences might include words in parenthesis - in brackets - a means of adding an extra point that is not essential to the sense of the sentence and yet which, precisely because it is enclosed in brackets, is given extra emphasis.

Punctuation

Questions on punctuation are likely to ask you about the use that the writer has made of commas, colons, semi-colons, parenthesis, question marks explanation marks or ellipsis so make sure that you know what the purposes of these punctuation marks are and how they relate to the structure of sentences.

Tone

In the context of written English language use, tone is short for tone of voice and is concerned with the fine distinctions in meaning or connotations that can occur between one word and another. Tone often reveals the writer's attitude to issues.

If, for example, you came across two writers who were debating the pros and cons of shopping and one made comments about people being 'addicted to shopping' while the other spoke of 'retail therapy' what would you take to be the different attitudes of the two writers to the shopping experience? And how would you know?

It sounds as if one writer is against people spending lots of time shopping and uses the word 'addicted' to suggest that such people are like drug addicts – not an image that we associate with healthy pursuits. The other writer, however, uses the word 'therapy' and this suggests approval of shopping as the word makes us think of a cure for ill-health or misfortune.

A writer might also use very *emotional* words to convey how much he/she cares about the issue in question. I am *devoted* to shopping, for example, is much stronger than I *like* shopping (You can see the connection here between tone and word choice) On the other hand, a writer might write in a very *ironic* or *sarcastic* way about something.

In an essay called, *A Modest Proposal*, Jonathan Swift, writer of *Gulliver's Travels* once suggested that poverty and famine in Ireland could easily be reduced if only parents sold off their too-numerous children to the gentry who could then eat them. Job done, as they say! In the event, his 'straight-faced' attack on the typical racist attitudes of the time towards the Irish was so sustained that some people thought that he was being serious and demanded that he be arrested and charged with incitement. Fortunately others recognised the essay as one of the most brilliant examples of satire ever written.

Further on tone, a writer might adopt a light-hearted or humorous attitude towards his or her topic as a means of engaging the interest of the reader. Use of *hyperbole* (exaggeration) or even *colloquial* or *slang* language in a passage that otherwise is full of formal English helps to achieve an amusing or tongue-in-cheek effect.

The final question on the prose passages in the CfE Higher English exam deals with tone and the attitudes of writers towards their subject so we return to this topic when we discuss evaluation.

Samples of questions and answers on identifying and analysing techniques

Read the following adapted extract from the introduction to this guide and then answer the questions on word choice, imagery, sentence structure and tone which follow. Questions here do not necessarily reflect the format used in the exam but they are designed to focus your attention on the various techniques that writers use to put over their message and that have just been discussed.

'Given the limited amount of available time, an examination can only ever test a small sample of your overall English skills - the literary skills that you <u>display</u> (have) when it comes to composing written work of your own and the literacy skills that help you to read, understand and write about the work of others.

So you need to answer questions as fully and as relevantly as possible in the time available.

It is a little like having all the knowledge, skills and commitment that you need to fill a post for which you have applied - and then not getting the job because you failed to communicate (state) those attributes fully enough on the day to the interview panel. To put it another way, an exam is a snapshot of your skills. You want to make sure that the snapshot catches you looking your best.

Looking your best in an exam requires you to call upon a range (number) of strategic, tactical and operational study skills that are not quite the same as the literary and literacy skills that are the marks of an English scholar (person). Strategic study skills are concerned with your overall longer term planning on how to demonstrate your literary and literacy skills under examination conditions; tactical skills are concerned with the way you prioritise your use of study time for examinations; and operational skills are concerned with the way you make best use of the time available to answer questions on the day to score the highest marks possible.

This Guide cannot improve your literary or literacy skills overnight. Such skills are developed over a lifetime (long time) as a result of reading and writing, talking and listening. Hopefully, too, they have been developed throughout the course of your studies in English. But the wealth of practical advice that the guide offers about <u>tackling</u> (doing) every part of the exam, together with the detailed sample answers, will help you to ensure that the sample of your literary and literacy skills that you present for assessment on exam day is your best sample.'

Question on word choice: Look at the six words that have been underlined in the extract above and then followed by a bracketed equivalent. Take each word in its turn and explain why it might be a better choice of word than its bracketed alternative.

Question on imagery: Identify from the first three paragraphs two images that are used by the writer to convey an important point about the nature of exams. Explain how the images help the writer to make his point more effectively.

Question on sentence structure and punctuation: Look at the sentence which begins 'Strategic study skills...' and explain how the structure and punctuation of that sentence emphasises the points being made.

Question on tone: Select a phrase from the first paragraph that conveys the writer's attitude to the value of exams and two phrases from the final paragraph that convey the attitude of the writer towards the value of his guide. Explain how the words help to convey the attitudes in question.

Sample answers
Word choice
'Display' suggests the ability to demonstrate your abilities in writing and not just have them; 'communicate' suggests again the ability actually to get your point over - you may state something with nobody hearing or understanding you;' 'range' suggests a wide variety of skills, a breadth of talent whereas 'number' may suggest some but not varied; 'scholar' suggests an intelligent person whereas 'person' suggests an ordinary person; "lifetime' suggests learning from your very earliest childhood years in a way that 'long time' does not; 'tackling' suggests that you are making a strong effort to deal with the questions, like a rugby player making a tackle to win the ball whereas 'doing' suggests a standard effort.

Imagery
'Sample' is a metaphor where the writer emphasises the small amount of your ability that is tested by comparing it to the 'sample' or small amount of material that a doctor or scientist might use to test something; 'snapshot' suggests that your ability is being tested at one moment in time in rather the

same way as a camera captures your looks at one moment in time.

Sentence structure and punctuation
The long sentence which begins 'Strategic study skills...' consists of three related sections that deal with strategic, tactical and operational skills in their turn. This list of skills is separated by semi-colons that invite you to pause for emphasis of each skill. The long sentence suggests the long periods of study required. The sentence builds up to a climax that throws great emphasis on the final point about scoring the highest marks possible.

Tone
The adverbs 'only ever', together with the adjective 'small' emphasise the writer's view that exams are limited in what they can test as they can only assess the answers you give and can never assess the answers you might have given. 'Wealth of practical advice' suggests the very great amount of high quality advice the guide offers - advice that you can actually use and not just think about; 'detailed sample answers' again suggests that the answers are very specific and relevant to the advice that has been given about how to answer different types of question.

Questions that invite you to evaluate how effectively the writer has used a technique

Such questions permeate every part of the CfE Higher English paper, explicitly or implicitly. Thus, in the case of the *Portfolio* you are by implication being invited to evaluate your own efforts to write effectively about your chosen creative and discursive topics as you draft and redraft your submissions.

The *Critical Writing* paper will explicitly invite you to comment extensively on the effectiveness with which an author has written a play, poem or novel. At the same time, you are implicitly invited to evaluate the clarity and coherence with which you compose your answers. In all of this, an extremely important skill is being tested – the skill to be able to express your *personal reactions* to the work of others and the skill to *evaluate* your own work. We say again, this is the skill above all other skills that a written exam tests.

In the *UAE* paper, you can expect to be invited not only to *understand* or *analyse* a point but to be able to comment on its effectiveness from your point of view. Watch out for questions that might invite you to analyse *and* evaluate the writer's use of technique. You cannot score full marks for such questions if you fail to *evaluate* as well as *analyse* the writer's use of language.

Suppose, for example, you had been asked to evaluate the effectiveness of the paragraph in the extract above that began, 'So you need to answer...'

You might have said something like: *This very short paragraph has only one sentence so the point about answering questions stands out. The conjunction 'so' suggests that this paragraph should just have been part of the previous sentence. But then the point would not have stood out so well. I think that important individual words like 'need', 'fully', 'relevantly' and 'time' get extra emphasis because the paragraph is so* short.

The comparison question

The final question in the *UAE paper* involves a particular kind of evaluation. In essence you are invited to evaluate the quality of writing in the two passages by *identifying, summarising* and *comparing* the key points and the *attitude* of the writers of the two passages as they address the given topic. Identifying, summarising comparing - no wonder this question is so hard!

Sometimes the viewpoints adopted will be the same but sometimes the viewpoints will be diametrically opposed to one another. Sometimes there might be a mixture of both. In essence, the ability that you are calling upon here is the ability to *summarise* and compare key points from two passages dealing with the same topic. Typically, the question is for *5 marks* and you want to make sure that you score as many of these as possible.

You may recall the earlier advice about briefly noting key points presented by the writer of the first passage as you work your way through the other questions.

It is now time for you to read the *second passage* and jot down key points as you go along. Typically, given the nature of the passages chosen by the examiner, you will be invited to identify up to five points where the two writers are in agreement or where they differ in their views or where there is a mixture of agreements and differences.

At the same time, you will be expected to refer to the words and phrases that indicate the *standpoints* of the writers and explain how these words do indeed convey a *point of view*.

Summarising key points from passages is very challenging as it is easy for you to be distracted by *repetitions* of points or *examples* of points, rather than the points themselves. Sometimes you might even have to *infer* or figure out key general points from the specific examples given. We come back to this later when we look at the *Specimen Paper*.

Specimen Higher English *UAE* paper

Specimen Question Papers are available at www.sqa.org.uk/pastpapers for all the new **National 5** and **Higher** Qualifications. Go to the web site, click or tap on 'Higher' for specimen question papers for the new Higher exams, scroll down the list of subjects to English and download the file called *English: Reading for Understanding, Analysis and Evaluation Specimen Question Paper Higher.*

The two specimen *UAE* passages deal with the importance of trees. Answer the questions *under examination timing* and see if you can score full marks, using all the advice you have been given. Other students have succeeded so why not you? Ask your teacher if he or she would be kind enough to mark your efforts.

Even better, check your answers against the sample answers, also provided by *SQA in that same downloaded file,* and score yourself according to the marking instructions. Analyse where and why you scored less than you might have done so that next time you will score full marks.

A complete set of sample answers by one individual to the Specimen *UAE* paper follows. Use the SQA specimen marking instructions to mark these sample answers - but only after you have had a go at answering the questions yourself. No cheating!

Specimen CfE Higher English UAE Paper: Draft answers
Question 1:

(a) The writer feels guilty about ordering the cutting down of a tree in her garden and wonders if she had the right to do it. But at the same time she feels justified about cutting the

tree down because it is too big and is cutting out the light.

(b) The writer uses the word 'precious' to emphasise that she thinks that trees are very important in our lives and deserve care; she contrasts their stability with the word 'steady' compared to all the changes or 'churning' that is going on elsewhere in the world; she uses the simile 'like God's arm" to suggest that trees give us life as God gives Adam life in the famous Sistine Chapel painting; she uses the simile and alliteration in 'calming like a cathedral' to emphasise how trees can soothe us when we are worried or upset.

Question 2
The protestors are not drop-outs or social outcasts who are fighting against unnecessary changes in the environment just for the sake of it. They are ordinary men, women and children who are honestly worried about the destruction that is being caused.

Question 3
(i) The writer uses three very short sentences in a row to emphasise how little time there is left even to slow down the development

(ii) The writer says 'By March' because the specific date emphasises again how time to save the situation is short

(iii) She uses the word 'dubious' to emphasise by understatement that she thinks

there will be no economic benefit from the project.

(iv) She uses the phrase 'boarded-up premises' to emphasise by her use of sarcasm how pointless the project is.

Question 4

(a) The government says that the protestors are not trying to protect the countryside. All they care about is their own comforts and well-being and not the needs of families who are poorer than they are.

(b) She says that cutting down trees is' 'brutal' and 'grotesque'. These are very strong emotional words and emphasise her belief in conservation by contrast with such destruction; she uses the similes 'like shooting an elephant or harpooning a whale' to emphasise that great trees, like these great creatures, need to be saved from extinction; her use of the phrase 'aching poignancy' suggests that she is so full of sympathy for the trees that it hurts her physically.

Question 5

(a) Trees can cause instability in the ground where houses stand; they can cause injury and so are a danger to health; their falling leaves and the fluids that come from them can cause a mess and damage people's possessions; some trees are very old-fashioned and should be replaced with more modern and unusual varieties.

(b) The writer uses a metaphor to compare the cutting down of the trees by council workers with a butcher hacking at meat with a cleaver. There is a feeling of great violence in these words and in that image that emphasises the brutality of the whole process.

Question 6
The final paragraph effectively sums up the points that the writer has been making throughout the passage - that trees make a valuable contribution to our lives and our world; that there may be no financial benefit in destroying them; that it seems inevitable that they will continue to be cut down anyway in the name of progress.

Question 7
Both writers agree that:

1. Trees deserve our respect: the first writer speaks of a branch of a tree being like God's arm reaching out to give life; the second writer speaks of the 'sheer gravitas' or serious importance of trees

2. They teach us to value stability and history: the first writer says trees are 'our living past" and speaks of their steadiness or stability in a 'churning' or changing world; the second writer explains the great age of the kauri tree and points out that these trees have outlasted extinct creatures

3. Ordinary people realise this and value trees: the first writer pays respect to ordinary

families and 'grandmothers' protesting about a road-building project that is destroying ancient woodland; the second writer respects folk in different parts of the world who conserve trees and even replant them

4.   Authorities are arrogant and brutal: the first writer speaks of the 'special kind of arrogance' of the authorities and of their butchering of trees; the second writer talks of the 'conceit' of authorities who think cutting down trees is progress and of the brutal 'hacking and racking' of trees

5.   Any economic gain from cutting down trees may be achieved at a greater loss: the first writer describes trees as being 'precious and 'beyond price'; the second writer points to the economic wisdom of tree-based farming.

Conclusion

Every time you read a piece of English writing from now on, it is suggested that you should get into the habit of asking yourself four questions:

1. What is this writer saying?
2. Which literary techniques are being used to put over points?
3. How effective are these techniques in putting points over?
4. How precise are my answers to these questions?

Part 3: Critical Reading

(a) Introduction

The *Critical Reading* paper tests your ability to express in writing your *understanding, analysis* and *evaluation* of at least two works of literature from the wide range that you will no doubt have explored with your teacher during your course of studies. It also tests your ability to compose *coherent* and *technically sound* critical essays.

One of the works must be taken from a reasonably wide list of pre-set Scottish texts (See the *SQA* for details of the set authors and texts each year) The first section of the *Critical Reading* paper invites you to analyse, by answering a series of questions, the content and style of an *extract* from one of your chosen texts before inviting you to analyse content and style elsewhere in the writer's work.

The second section of the *Critical Reading* paper invites you to write a critical essay in which you demonstrate your appreciation of any other work of literature so long as it is from a different genre from the extract that you chose in section 1. This section not only tests your ability to *understand*, *analyse* and *evaluate* a piece of work (as in the *UAE paper*) but also your ability to compose coherent extended writing (as in the *portfolio*)

Revisit www.sqa.org.uk/pastpapers and download the file *English: Critical Reading Specimen Question Paper Higher* for an example of the new format. Remember you have to analyse only *one* extract and then write only *one* critical essay from the range available. So don't panic!

(b) Timing
Each of the two sections is marked out of 20 and the total marks account for the remaining 40% of the total. So it is recommended that you allocate *45 minutes* to each section of the paper. It might be an idea to write your traditional critical essay *first* before addressing the questions on the extract from your set text. Be careful, however, not to spend so much time on your critical essay that you do not have time left to do justice to the questions on the set text extract and in particular the last question on that extract where up to ten marks are available for a series of points about the writer's work overall.

(c) Criteria
The criteria for critical essays are again concerned with your level of ability to *understand, analyse* and *evaluate* the text about which you are writing. You need also to *compose* a coherent essay that satisfies high standards of spelling, punctuation and logical flow. A good answer will satisfy the following:
- There is a good knowledge and understanding of the contents of the text
- The question is answered fully with plenty of relevant evidence to support points

- There is a sophisticated awareness of literary and linguistic techniques
- Personal opinions about the quality of the text are clearly expressed

d) Meeting the criteria
Planning, prioritising, writing answers
Part 3d (i): Planning
Planning to deal in the exam with the two sections of the *Critical Reading* paper is essentially concerned with *immersing* yourself as fully as possible in all the texts that you liked so much that you would like to focus upon them in the exam.

It is a good idea to jot down as you read a favourite text any thoughts that you may have, or explanations that your teacher may give you, about parts of the text that particularly please you. Then *memorise* not only sections of the text but the points that you would like to make about it.

Clearly, you are likely to focus on studying texts that have been selected by your teacher but just as your teacher will probably select texts from his or her favourite works of literature, you too must make the final decision as to the texts that you like. There is nothing harder than trying to write fully and enthusiastically in an exam about a text that you did not enjoy or even understand, But do seek your teacher's advice on this important matter.

Part 3d (ii): Prioritising

One of the texts or group of texts that you must deal with in the exam comes from a prescribed list of Scottish authors. The list is reviewed and revised every three years so clearly it is important for you to be aware of the authors on the list in any given year.

Given the fact that questions in that part of the *Critical Reading* paper focus on a short extract from one of the prescribed texts, you can safely assume that your teacher will focus in some detail on one play, one novel or one group of poems or short stories from the prescribed list.

The list features works that have become favourites and are of a high enough quality to merit their selection. But if the selection chosen by your teacher is not attractive to you then you have a decision to make – either to try as hard as possible to find and learn the merits of the text in question or to study your own preferred selection, seeking advice and guidance from your teacher as you go along.

There is also a pragmatic point to consider - the forty five minutes that you have available for each answer to demonstrate your levels of literary appreciation in a way that meets the criteria for a top mark. The time available to answer questions fully on an extract from your chosen Scottish text may lead you to select a group of poems or short stories as it then becomes possible for you to remember more or less everything about the texts in question.

Alternatively, you will probably find yourself focusing as you prepare for your exam on at least two characters and perhaps two key scenes from your chosen play or novel.

The same pragmatic considerations will apply to the texts that you decide to focus on in the other section of the *Critical Reading* paper – always remembering, of course, that you are required to select texts from the two sections of the paper from different genres.

Reading for pleasure and reading to do well in an exam is not always the same thing. You may well decide that reading to do well in the exam is your priority at this stage of your education. In that case, make it a priority to draft and redraft practice answers to different questions on your favourite texts from the past papers until you have identified the limits to what you can remember and the number of words you can write in forty five minutes. If this seems like lots of hard and possibly boring work, that's because it is. But keep your eye on the prize – a top score in your Higher English exam - and you will be encouraged to stick to your task. It is not as if it is mission impossible.

Part 3d (iii): Answering questions

The critical essay section of the Critical Reading paper, as you can see from the **English: Critical Reading Specimen Paper Higher** at the SQA past papers web site, provides you typically with three questions from each of the genres of drama, poetry, fiction prose, non-fiction prose, film and TV and language. Questions are fairly 'open-ended' in that they fit a variety of texts. But do be aware that they will be 'closed' in that they will invite you to focus on a specific aspect or part or feature of a text. There is not much sense in telling your marker all about your favourite *character* in *The Great Gatsby* or whatever when the question is about the *setting* of the novel.

Remember, again, that if you decide to focus on, say, poetry, for your set text question then you cannot choose to write a critical essay on poetry. So cover your bets! You would be wise to *immerse* yourself in at least the following: two main *characters* and a key *scene* from your favourite play; two main *characters* and a key *incident* from your favourite novel; at least *two* poems from your favourite poet. As an alternative to (or an addition to) a novel, you might immerse yourself in at least one *short story and* one *non-fiction* essay. Steer clear of film, TV and Language options unless you have explored these options in some detail as part of your course.

By all means, use analyses and notes by others to help you to understand literature – just so long as you remember that your marker will not be impressed if the views you express in the exam are someone else's and patently not yours. Markers are remarkably adept at spotting candidates who plagiarise the views of others while not having a clue about the texts they claim to love so much. Sincere personal reactions to texts carry a very great deal of weight with markers, especially if they have just read half a dozen different answers from half a dozen different candidates that all look as if they were written by the one person!

The second most important point to make is that no question will ever invite you to write down everything that you can think of about any play, poem or novel that you have studied. Immersing yourself in the details of your chosen texts ahead of the exam is one thing; blanket coverage of a text in an answer, with little or no reference to the question that was asked, is a serious no-no. So read questions carefully before picking one that will allow you to write about your chosen text in a way that is *relevant* to the demands of the question.

Do spend a moment or two on this. You may very well be in a position to tackle several of the options on offer and you want to choose the one that offers you the best chance of scoring top marks.

Each question comes in three parts to reflect the recurring requirement to demonstrate in your answers the ability to *understand*, *analyse* and *evaluate* your chosen text or texts. First you will be invited to select a text, or section of a text, that deals with a certain theme or topic. The question will also require you *briefly* to sum up key points about the topic. Then you will be invited to *analyse* and *evaluate* in some detail, and with close reference to the text, the ways in which the author communicates his or her 'message' - *to you*.

Take careful note of the boxed advice that is offered with each genre. It relates to features that are typical of a given genre and will help you to make sure that you comment on a wide range of relevant features. Re-checking the words of the question occasionally will also help to ensure that you are answering the question that was asked and not the one you wanted to be asked!

Examples of critical essays

The essays that follow are examples of how you might analyse a text of your choice in a suitably relevant way. They are responses to questions that have been asked in *Specimen Papers* for the new format of the Higher English Critical Reading paper.

Each answer reflects the very great deal of preparation that was undertaken in advance by the writers to familiarise themselves thoroughly with their chosen texts so that they could write at considerable length within the forty five minutes available for each question. And even although they may make points that other people could also make, you should be able to detect the signs that indicate that these are *personal* reactions. As you read them, judge for yourself the relevance of the answers to the questions being asked.

Critical Essay (1)
Specimen question: Select a play that has an important turning point. Briefly describe what happens at the turning point and by referring to important techniques show how the turning point impacts on the play as a whole?

Your first step is to the question.

The question requires the candidate to:

a) Select a turning point in a play and summarise what happens at this turning point

b) Explain how the turning point impacts upon the play as a whole

c) Refer to appropriate techniques used by the playwright to emphasise the importance of the turning point for the play as a whole.

The overall answer should comprise:

S – Selection of the points about the text that the candidate wishes to make

Q – Quotes from the piece of writing to illustrate the points being made

A – Analysis and evaluation of the quotes to demonstrate that the candidate understands and is affected by the writer's craft

You might find the mnemonic useful!

Dramatic techniques

Dramatic techniques refer to the various ways in which a playwright seeks to grip the attention of an audience and to get across his 'message' as clearly and as effectively as possible. Remember that a play is performed in some kind of theatre for an audience and so some of the theatrical techniques are specific to drama as a genre. Others are concerned with *what* the characters say and do and *how* they say and do it (publicly and privately). Below are some of the techniques used by Shakespeare in *Macbeth, Act 1 scene 7*, where there is an important turning point.

1. The very *placing* of the scene at the end of Act 1 emphasises that a climax has been reached.

2. The use of *compressed time* to speed up the action and to make the story unfold in a speedy and exciting way. One moment Macbeth decides not to proceed with his plan to kill Duncan, the next he decides that he will go ahead. The speed of events helps to emphasise the power and influence that Lady Macbeth has over her husband at this stage.

3. The use of *soliloquy* (where the stage is occupied by a single character who is reflecting out loud on his or her private thoughts and feelings) allows us to see what Macbeth is thinking and feeling and to understand the contrast between his public face and his private attitudes. The use of brief

asides (although not used in Act 1, scene 7) serve a similar purpose. The first major *soliloquy* of the play occurs in Act 1, scene 7. What does it reveal about Macbeth that is new?

4. *Dramatic irony* – where the words that characters use have a greater ironic significance for the audience than they do for the characters in question. There is an excellent example of *visual irony* in Act 1, scene 7. Macbeth says he has 'no spur to prick the side of his intent' to murder Duncan. At this very moment, in walks Lady Macbeth and we soon realise that here is a spur that Macbeth was not thinking about. What other examples of irony are there in that scene?

5. The use of *contrast* – both *between* characters and the changing nature *within* characters to emphasise what people are like. Clear contrasts between Macbeth and Lady Macbeth in Act 1, scene 7. Contrasts in their changing nature and changing relationship are also *foreshadowed* (See below) in much of what is said in Act 1, scene 7.

6. The use of *foreshadowing* – words or actions that point the audience towards comments and actions that are to come along later. Many examples in Act 1, Scene 7. In essence, the decision to proceed with the murder of Duncan foreshadows all that is to come: the murder of Duncan and the grooms, the flight of Malcolm and Macduff to lead the eventual rebellion against Macbeth, the

murder of Banquo and of Macduff's family, the growing amorality of Macbeth and his eventual death at the hands of Macduff and the gradual decline of Lady Macbeth.

7. The use of *poetic techniques* such as metaphor and simile, rhythm and rhyme to make points in a striking and memorable way. Many examples in Act 1, scene 7, especially in connection with the emotional state that Macbeth is in and the calculated emotions, by contrast, of Lady Macbeth.

Having taken the trouble to study a range of dramatic techniques, do remember to read over the boxed advice which lists the kinds of techniques to which you might refer.

It is then a good idea to take the words of the question and to use them to compose an opening statement that indicates clearly that you intend to identify and then summarise a turning point.

The next step is to outline how this turning point impacts upon the rest of the play as a whole. This will involve you in comparing and contrasting what has been going on up until this point with what happens after this point.

Thereafter, you will be focusing on the techniques and features that Shakespeare uses to show how important this scene is to the play as a whole.

Sample answer

A play with an important turning point is 'Macbeth' by William Shakespeare. The turning point occurs in Act 1, scene 7. Driven by his own ambitious desires, encouraged by the earlier prophesies of the three witches, and stung by the accusation of his wife, Lady Macbeth, that he is a coward, Macbeth finally resolves to kill King Duncan and seize the throne of Scotland. Inevitably, this decision impacts upon everything that happens in the rest of the play, not least the series of tragic events that are to follow.

At the beginning of the scene we see Macbeth alone on the stage with his thoughts about the possibility of becoming king of Scotland by force. He summarises all the reasons for not killing King Duncan.

At this point, Lady Macbeth arrives and Macbeth tells her that he wishes to 'proceed no further in this business' – the proposal to murder Duncan.

Lady Macbeth launches an attack upon her husband and accuses him of being a coward. He hesitates and she presses on by proposing a plan whereby they can kill Duncan and blame the murder on his attendants. Dominated by Lady Macbeth as he is, and with his ambition blinding him to the flaws in her plan, Macbeth agrees that they will go ahead with the murder after all. 'I am settled', he says.

In my opinion, the scene marks a major turning point in Macbeth's character and in his relationship with his wife, Lady Macbeth. In the early moments of the scene, he demonstrates to us that he still has some sense of morality. As he reminds us himself, this is a man who has won great respect from everyone from Duncan down to the soldiers in the field for his courage, his military skills and his loyalty. Now, in his resentment at his wife's accusation of cowardice and, by his own admission, he reveals the tragic flaws in his character, the pride and the 'vaulting ambition', that is eventually to bring about his destruction.

We have seen Macbeth swithering in the earlier scenes about how, if at all, he might become king. Perhaps the throne might even become his by chance, until Duncan nominates his son Malcolm as his successor and forces Macbeth to think the unthinkable. But from now on, he is much more decisive. He goes ahead with the murder of Duncan as planned. And he calmly murders the king's attendants before fixing the blame on them. Although his conscience throws up images of daggers and sleepless nights before and after the murder of Duncan, he steadily becomes more and more callous He coolly plans the murder of Banquo and his son Fleance so that Banquo's family will not one day inherit the throne, as the witches had promised. When the appearance of the ghost of Banquo exposes his guilt, he deliberately seeks out the witches for further prophecies about his future and, encouraged by their ambiguous assurances, he coldly plans to murder

Macduff. When Macduff escapes, Macbeth ruthlessly has his family slaughtered. Eventually, he dies at the hands of Macduff, with only his former bravery intact. Each event follows almost inevitably from the previous one.

The scene also marks the high point of Lady Macbeth's control over her husband. I think, in all probability, he would not have gone ahead with the murder of Duncan without her biting attack on his courage. From now on, however, he increasingly comes to his own decisions. It is he who commits the murder and not Lady Macbeth, for all her hardness of heart. And she knows nothing of his plan to murder Banquo and Fleance. She is unable to control her husband's ravings at the appearance of Banquo's ghost in the banquet scene that was supposed to celebrate Macbeth's accession to the throne. Again, she knows nothing of the plan to murder Macduff and, when she hears of the slaughter of his wife and children by her husband, the knowledge helps to drive her into the madness and despair that leads to her eventual suicide. I feel sorrier for her than Macbeth.

Above all, the scene marks a major turning point in Macbeth's scope for free will. Until now, he has options that he can select from. Despite the influence of the witches and his wife, he still does not have to kill Duncan. But with the decision to go ahead with the crime,

Macbeth increasingly finds himself being controlled by events. He feels that he has no choice but to kill Banquo if he is to keep the ill-gotten crown. He also feels compelled to seek out the witches for further reassurance after the appearance of Banquo's ghost. He feels compelled to try and destroy Macduff when his spies let him know that Macduff is ready to lead a rebellion against his rule. And in the end, he has no choice but to fight for his life, a losing fight as it turns out.

Shakespeare uses a range of techniques to emphasise how this scene makes an important impact on the play as a whole. These include the placing of the scene and the use of soliloquy, character contrast, dramatic irony, foreshadowing, compressed time and a range of powerful images.

Shakespeare emphasises the importance of this scene by placing it at the end of Act 1. This helps us to realise that a major climax has been reached, in this case the decision to go ahead with the murder of Duncan after a great deal of indecision.

We are also presented with the first soliloquy in the play. Macbeth is on stage alone so we are focused on him and his private thoughts. In earlier scenes, we had gathered that Macbeth was 'valour's minion', 'Bellona's bridegroom and a 'worthy gentleman'. But we had also learned from a series of asides from him that he had secret ambitions for the crown and was excited by the prophecy of the witches that he would one day be king. Now as he explores his mixed emotions before us, we realise that this is a man with a moral flaw. Even the reasons he provides for not killing Duncan are more about the practicalities than they are about the fundamental amorality of such an act. But at least he does initially come to the right decision. 'We shall proceed no further in this business' he tells his wife who has just arrived.

Dramatic irony is used to signal to us the importance of her arrival. Macbeth has just concluded that he has 'no spur to prick the side of my intent' except 'vaulting ambition'. At this very moment, Lady Macbeth enters and we realise that here is a major 'spur' to push him on, one that is every bit as important as his ambition.

We are focused for the remainder of the scene on these two major characters and the contrasts between them. Her powerful attack on his reasons for not killing Duncan balances his reasons for not going ahead and emphasises just how callous she is compared to him at this stage. As we heard earlier, she thinks her husband is 'too full o' the milk o' human kindness.' Her charge of cowardice makes it clear how well she knows her husband and how to manipulate him. 'I dare do all that may become a man', he says. His reply to her attack emphasises just how much he admires her and is dominated by her. He praises her 'undoubted mettle.' The speed with which he changes his mind and decides to proceed with the murder emphasises the degree of control that she has over him at this point but also indicates that, despite his earlier decision to proceed no further, he is still driven by ambition.

At the same time, the scene foreshadows a major change in the relationship between the two. Macbeth is indeed 'settled' and having made his mind up finally goes on to dominate their relationship. Lady Macbeth by contrast becomes increasingly horrified by the actions of the monster that she has unleashed and the horrific slaughter of Macduff's family in particular drives her to insanity.

Shakespeare uses a series of powerful images throughout the scene to emphasise the contrast between the two characters. For example, Macbeth's image of how Duncan's worthiness will 'plead like angels' if he is killed and how pity for him will be 'like a new-born babe', or 'heaven's cherubim' conveys the mixture of feelings he is going through at this point. By contrast, the image of Lady Macbeth dashing out the brains of her own baby rather than go back on the oath she has sworn to kill Duncan is the clearest possible indication of her callous cruelty at this point. How ironic is it that one day it will be the murder of Macduff's children that helps to drive her insane. And how ironic it is that she thinks that it is Duncan's guards 'who shall bear the guilt of our great quell.' The scene ends with a statement from Macbeth that sums up much of the hypocrisy that is to come:

False face must hide what the false heart doth know.

By using all these dramatic techniques, Shakespeare helps us to realise just how important this scene is in the play as a turning point and its impact on the play as a whole. (approx 1550 words)

This is a much longer answer than you could write out in 45 minutes. But I have deliberately made it very full so that you can see what a first draft, composed with no time pressures, might look like. You should try to write down a version of this in no more than 45 minutes so that you will know just how much you can write in that amount of time.

So long as you know your material well enough, you should be able to write up to *1000* legible words per essay in the time available (around *22* words per minute) unless, of course, there are special circumstances in your case.

Once you have drawn up a first draft answer to the question, you should work through it point by point and picking out the points that make most sense to you so that you end up with a version that answers the question very thoroughly in your own words.

As always, the important thing at this stage of the proceedings is to practise past paper questions as much as possible and learn material off by heart ahead of the exam so that you are able to write a great deal of relevant comment even under the pressure of time. So sorry to be giving you what looks like hard work again – but it is actually SMART work. Everything to do with your pre-exam studies in *critical reading* should be focused on providing Specific, Measurable, Achievable, Relevant and Timed answers.

Critical Essay (2)

Specimen question: Choose a play in which the conflict between two characters is an important feature. Briefly explain the nature of the conflict and discuss how the dramatist's presentation of this feature enhances your understanding of the play as a whole.

Sample answer

A play in which the conflict between two characters is an important feature is 'Macbeth' by William Shakespeare. The conflict is between Macbeth himself and his wife, Lady Macbeth. At the heart of the conflict is a debate between them about what, if anything, should be done about the prophecy by some witches that Macbeth will one day be king of Scotland.

As the conflict unfolds, we see its serious consequences not just for the two central characters but for the country as a whole. And as they and their relationship changes, we understand more and more clearly the central 'message' of the play - that power corrupts and absolute power corrupts absolutely.

Briefly, Macbeth is an initially loyal and courageous nobleman who, because of his 'vaulting ambition', becomes increasingly determined to seize and retain the throne of Scotland. Lady Macbeth, for her part, seems initially to be even more determined to ensure that her husband is successful in his ambition, and seems in the beginning to be even more cruel than her husband is in her determination that King Duncan, the rightful king, must die. It is the series of clashes between these two that enhances our understanding of how a craze for power can destroy not only individuals but also relationships and even whole countries if the protagonists are significant enough.

We first see the two together after Macbeth, one of the right hand men of Duncan, king of Scotland, has defeated two different foes in the one day and has been admired amongst the other lords for his bravery and loyalty. Even before we meet him, we hear of him being described as 'valour's minion' and 'Bellona's bridegroom'. Duncan himself calls him 'noble Macbeth' and 'peerless kinsman' and values his loyalty.

But Macbeth has a darker side. He is stopped by three strange witches as he travels home from battle with his great friend

Banquo and is told by them that he is to become Thane of Cawdor and king thereafter. His reaction to this prophecy is revealing to say the least.

'Why do you start and seem to fear things that do sound so fair', Banquo asks him.

When the news comes that Duncan has indeed appointed Macbeth as Thane of Cawdor, Macbeth is clearly 'rapt' as he thinks about the possibility of the kingship. Initially, Macbeth assumes that he may gain the throne by chance as he is a kinsman but when Duncan announces that his son, Malcolm will succeed him, Macbeth reveals to us in an aside his 'black and deep desires'.

Yet from Lady Macbeth's point of view, as we gather when first we see her alone, her husband, although he is not 'without ambition' is 'without the illness that should attend it'. She thinks that he is ' too full o' the milk of human kindness'. What he prizes 'highly', he still wants 'holily', so far as she is concerned.

When Lady Macbeth receives her husband's letter concerning the prophecies, and news of Duncan's impending arrival on a visit to their castle, she cannot wait to take over the planning of his murder. She prays to be filled with 'direst cruelty' and tells her husband upon his arrival that he must put the night's 'great dispatch' - the murder of Duncan - into her hands. Macbeth, for his part, seems to hesitate - ' we shall speak further', he says. So far then, Macbeth, unlike his wife, seems hesitant, although tempted by his wife's strong encouragement. He also comes across as a man with some virtues, unlike his wife who seems to have none. Their next meeting is crucial.

In the scene that significantly ends Act 1 of the play, the conflict between them reaches its head. As Macbeth himself reveals in his first soliloquy, he knows that there will be consequences if he kills the king and that murder cannot be 'the be-all and end-all'. He knows he should show loyalty to a much-loved king who is also his kinsman. He admits to himself and to us that he is driven by 'vaulting ambition' but at this stage he still has some sense of duty and loyalty and tells Lady Macbeth when she arrives that he will 'proceed no further' with the proposal to murder Duncan.

Lady Macbeth wants Macbeth to succeed and wants to see his ambition fulfilled. She knows that he would never kill the king of his own accord, and so she starts taunting Macbeth's masculinity, teasing out his weakness, forcing him act on it:

"What beast was it then that made you break this enterprise to me?

When you durst do it, then you were a man"

Lady Macbeth knows that deep inside Macbeth there is great ambition and power lust, but in order to tap into this inner cold-bloodedness, he must lose any human compassion.

Her statement that she would rather dash her baby's brains out than change her mind about killing Duncan shocks him. She calls him a coward and the insult to his warrior pride leads to his decision to kill the king after all. 'I am settled', he says.

We know from his earlier asides and his conversations with Banquo that, unlike him, Macbeth has been fascinated with the prophecies of the witches. And it seems clear that he has harboured ambitions for some time. But it is this argument with his wife that has brought matters to a head and has ended with his fateful decision to kill the king. It is that decision that changes everything from now on.

In the period ahead of the murder and for a short period afterwards, Macbeth reveals that he can still be conscience-stricken. But his determination to put out of his mind the vision of a blood-stained dagger that might have frightened him off from the murder reveals how desperate he is to become king.

He is also conscience-stricken after Duncan's murder. He 'shall sleep no more' and he is convinced that even 'Neptune's ocean' will never wash the blood from his hands. He refuses to return to the murder room to smear the king's servants with blood so that they will be blamed. His words to Lady Macbeth are revealing:

'I am afraid to think what I have done'

When there is suddenly a great knocking at the castle door, Macbeth says, in a way that reveals his torment: 'Wake Duncan with thy knocking! I would thou couldst.'

Yet Lady Macbeth remains icily cool - at least for the time being. 'Infirm of purpose', she snaps, and after smearing the grooms herself, she says, with dramatic irony, as she looks at her bloodied hands, 'a little water clears us of this deed'. She seems to lack insight.

But as time goes by, Macbeth becomes a changed man, now willing to slaughter anybody to achieve his goals. His cool planning of the murder of his friend Banquo and his son shows us how ruthless he has become. Banquo may suspect him of the king's murder and his descendants are promised the throne by the witches, leaving Macbeth with 'a fruitless' crown' so Banquo and his son must die. No conflict with Lady Macbeth now. In fact, Macbeth does not even tell his wife of his plan. ' Be innocent of the knowledge, dearest chuck', he says, 'til thou applaud the deed'.

Banquo is indeed murdered but the escape of Fleance leaves Macbeth feeling trapped, as his words reveal:

'I am cabinn'd cribb'd confined"

His hysterical reactions to the appearance of the ghost of Banquo at the great state banquet to celebrate his coronation as king reveals to all his guilt in Banquo's murder, despite the best efforts of Lady Macbeth to control the situation. This time her efforts to attack his manliness and stop his ravings come to nothing. 'I dare do all that may become a man', he says. His decision to revisit the witches for further reassurances lets us know that for him now there is no turning back.

"I am in blood stepped so far that I should wade no more,

Returning were as tedious as go'er"

Macbeth travels to where the witches live, hoping to find out more about his future. When they warn him about the threat of MacDuff, he immediately plans his death. And when MacDuff escapes, he immediately resolves to slaughter MacDuff's family:

"His wife, his babes and all unfortunate souls"

Macbeth again plans these murders and has them carried out without his wife's knowledge. Perhaps she would have opposed such a decision - and certainly these murders come back to haunt her - but she simply has no influence over her husband any more

Macbeth is now more ruthless than his wife ever was. From now on, as he says, 'the firstlings of my heart shall be the firstlings of my head.' The whole of Scotland is soon suffering from his tyranny. As the thane of Ross says, 'The dead man's knell is there scarce asked for who'.

Lady Macbeth is driven to madness with the guilt of her husband's mounting crimes and features less and less in her husband' life. She who once declared that 'a little water' would clear them of murder now says that all the perfumes of Arabia could not sweeten her hand. Insane with guilt, she commits suicide.

The news of Lady Macbeth's death affects Macbeth deeply and his words are those of a man who sees clearly how meaningless life has become – life is 'a tale, told by an idiot, signifying nothing'.

With the news that Malcolm, MacDuff and their army are at the very gates of his castle, there is nothing left for Macbeth but a final show of his bravery:

'At least we'll die with harness on our backs'.

And so we see how the conflict between Macbeth and his wife led to the decision to kill a king, to destroy their own happiness and to destroy almost a whole country. Such are the fruits of 'vaulting ambition'.

(Compare this similarly long answer to the previous one and you will see how you can adapt material that you know well to the question being asked)

The structure of poetry
If you choose to provide a critical essay on a poem then you will no doubt be focusing on how the author chooses words carefully and uses a series of striking images to put over

viewpoints in a vivid and memorable way. But you really should say a little about the structure of the poem and its rhythm and rhyme schemes and how the poet uses these to emphasise the key images even further. What follows is a brief summary of key points about the structure of poems.

In the same way that prose is written in paragraphs and songs are written in verses, so poems are written in *stanzas*. Normally each stanza deals with each new aspect of the given topic. Stanzas will be of different lengths, depending on the number of lines in each stanza. Normally, the stanzas within a given poem will all be the same length with each line following a given pattern. Poets may sometimes deliberately break up the regularity of their stanza lengths in order to emphasise some particular point.

Each line of a stanza consists of a given number of repeated *rhythms*. The commonest of all rhythms reflects the rhythm of a beating heart – *da* **dum**, *da* **dum**, *da* **dum,** *da* **dum**, *da* **dum**. Each single recurrence of this beat is called an *iamb*. If there are five beats to each line then this is called *iambic pentameter*. Iambic pentameter is the commonest type of line in all English poetry and provides a steady, stately kind of pace that can be varied to create even slower or sometimes faster speeds. Iambic tetrameter (four beats) for example, is quicker.

The opposite of an iamb is a trochee where the stress falls on the first syllable – **dum** *da*, **dum** *da*, **dum** *da*, **dum** *da*. Poets often use trochee to place emphasise on particular words that they want to highlight, thus again drawing attention to the meaning of the word or the image being used. A very good example is Blake's famous poem, 'The Tyger' which begins:

Tyger! Tyger! Burning bright

The way in which rhyming words are used in a poem also affects the speed of a poem. Alternating rhyming lines, where the last word of every second line rhymes, are like iambic pentameter in helping to convey a steadily paced unfolding event. Rhyming couplets, on the other hand, where the last words of each of two consecutive lines rhyme creates a sense of much more speed. Compare the following:

(a) The curfew tolls the knell of parting <u>day</u>   A
The lowing herd winds slowly o'er the <u>lea</u>   B
The ploughman homeward plods his weary <u>way.</u> A
And leaves the world to darkness and to <u>me</u>.   B

(b) As Tammie glowr'd, amaz'd, and <u>curious,</u>   A
The mirth and fun grew fast and <u>furious</u>;   A
The piper loud and louder <u>blew;</u>   B
The dancers quick and quicker <u>flew</u>;   B

They reel'd, they set, they cross'd, they <u>cleekit</u>,   C
Till ilka carlin swat and <u>reekit</u>,   C

And coost her duddies to the <u>wark</u>,   D
And linket at it in her <u>sark</u>!   D

The first extract is taken from a poem called 'Elegy in a Country Churchyard' by Thomas Gray and the second extract is taken from 'Tam O'Shanter' by Robert Burns. Gray's elegy reflects upon the worthiness but the anonymity of the lives of the humble country folk who are buried in a country church graveyard. Burns tells the merry tale of a drunken pedlar who stumbles across witches dancing at midnight in a ruined kirk.

The dark sombre mood of the first poem is in complete contrast to the cheerful merriment of the second. And this is emphasised by the contrasting rhythms and rhymes of each.

The elegy is written in iambic pentameter with alternating rhyme and Tam's story is told in iambic tetrameter with rhyming couplets. Read aloud both extracts and you should be able to hear how the slow iambic pentameter of the first, together with the alternating rhymes, establishes a slow movement and a sad mood that is emphasised by the alliteration, onomatopoeia and transferred epithet in for example:

'The <u>pl</u>ough man homeward <u>pl</u>ods his <u>w</u>eary <u>w</u>ay'

By contrast, the shorter iambic tetrameter with rhyming couplets of '*Shanter*' emphasises the fast action of that poem, as does the series of verbs.

In the case of poets such as Norman MacCaig who use free verse that does not follow any strict pattern, take note of how the poet may *break up* lines or *run on* lines in order to place greater emphasis on key words or points that he especially wishes to draw to our attention. Note also how a poet might vary the basics patterns that he has established in order to convey some change or disruption of the mood.

In conclusion, look at the basic line lengths, rhythms and rhymes of any poem and note how cleverly the poet uses them to emphasise the pace or mood of a poem or some particularly important point that the writer wishes to make.

The Sonnet Form

A sonnet is a short poem in which there is a particularly clear use of structure, rhyme and rhythm in order to point up key words or images that the poet wishes us to notice. A traditional sonnet is strictly limited to fourteen lines of iambic pentameters in which the writer usually explores two contrasting aspects about the nature of his love for someone.

The fourteen lines are divided into two groups – a group of eight lines (the 'octet' or sometimes two 'quatrains') and a group of six lines (the sestet). The rhyming scheme of the octet is ABBA, ABBA and the rhyming scheme of the sestet is usually CDCDCD (sometimes CDC, CDC)

Such rhyming schemes help the writer to emphasise the key words or ideas that are central to his or her overall 'message'. The ninth line in the overall group usually indicates some sort of turning point or change of point in the 'message' that the poet is trying to express in an effort to get across his mixed feelings about his subject.

Sonnets originated in Italy and their leading exponent was the Italian poet, Petrarch. Later they became very popular in England during Elizabethan times and their most famous exponent was Shakespeare. He varied the structure somewhat by dividing the fourteen lines into three groups of four lines (quatrains) and a concluding couplet. The rhyming scheme was typically ABAB, CDCD, EFEF for the quatrains and the final couplet rhymed GG.

The English language does not contain so many rhyming words as Italian so the rhyming scheme used by Shakespeare was easier to manage. But he retained iambic pentameter as before and the basic idea was still to express two or more key aspects of the love of a woman in an interesting and memorable way. The Shakespearean sonnet is often used to develop a sequence of metaphors or ideas, one in each quatrain, while the couplet offers either a summary or a new take on the preceding images or ideas.

Nowadays, poets are less keen on having to express their ideas while following a kind of structural formula (except those who like to tweet poems!) Yet, poets do sometimes use the sonnet form to explore different aspects of modern issues (not necessarily love themes) and often the mood can be dark as opposed to the lovestruck mood of the traditional sonnet.

A good example of this is Edwin Morgan's **Glasgow Sonnet (1)** where Morgan uses the traditional Petrarchan sonnet structure with its associations of love and beauty to explore, in an ironic way, different aspects of inner city decay and its impact on people's lives.

Invited by a specimen question to choose a poem that deals with *alienation*, and to show how the poet's exploration of the emotion had deepened understanding of it, a candidate wrote as follows:

Critical Essay (3)
Sample answer
Edwin Morgan explores alienation in "Glasgow Sonnets (1) by describing a crumbling and condemned Glasgow tenement and its depressing surroundings. He then focuses on the impact of this symbol of urban decay on the miserable lives of its last occupants, a poverty-stricken family who seem to be cut off from their right to a decent life.

The poet opens the poem by describing the exterior of the flats, going into detail about the filth of the place:

"A mean wind wanders"

The use of onomatopoeia and alliteration helps to emphasise the coldness, not only of the weather but also the depressing atmosphere of the situation. "backcourt trash" describes the dirtiness of the place, and emphasises the filthiness of the surroundings.

The poet continues this idea of dirtiness and filth when he describes what the children play with:

"Play-fortresses of bric-a-brac spill out some ash"

There is a hard sound to 'bric-a-brac' and 'ash' emphasises the filthy surroundings that the children have to defend themselves against even when playing in their 'fortresses'. Once again there is a feeling of hopelessness and depression. The overall setting suggests a context for life that is cut off from what should be normal amenities.

The poem then focuses on the building itself:

"Four storeys have no windows left to smash"

The vandalism gives an impression of a danger about the place. There is a feeling of violence in the word, 'smash'.

The next quote gives more information of the bad state the building is in:

"That black block condemned to stand, not crash"

"Black block" describes the unappealing architectural quality of the building, as well as a "block" being a term used to describe prison buildings. "Condemned to stand, not crash" tells us that it would actually be a positive event if the building was demolished, rather than have it standing, being a danger to the one family left to reside in it, and the building also being an eyesore. The whole setting feels quite outlandish.

The poet then turns to the interior of the last remaining occupied apartment:

"Roses of mould grow from ceiling to wall"

"Roses" makes us think of beautiful flowers and delicate plants, whereas here it is used to describe the mould that covers a whole portion of a room. It is in direct contrast to the rest of the poem, and it emphasises the hopelessness of the place, almost as if mould is the closest thing that they have to roses around the area. The fact that the mould is "from ceiling to wall" only places more emphasis on the dirtiness of the building. Not only that, but mould can destroy structures, so it is only putting the family in a more dangerous spot. Once again, there is an overall feeling of decay where there should be brightness.

The feeling of alienation is most powerfully conveyed, however, when the poet turns finally to the people who live in the flat:

"The man lies late since he has lost his job" this tells us that the man is in such a bad state of depression, that he cannot even motivate himself to get out of bed. He has lost his job,

132

meaning that he has little to no money for himself and his family. Another reason for him staying in bed is that the building is cold, so under the blankets must be some kind of semi-warm sanctuary.

"Smokes on one elbow, letting his coughs fall thinly into air too poor to rob": This tells us that he is in some kind of inner-turmoil, shown by the fact that he is smoking on his own, just lying down. Also, this shows that he is probably smoking to get rid of the pain of hunger, as smoking takes away your appetite. "Coughs fall" emphasises the depression and hopelessness of the man, "fall" connoting a lack of power or strength. "into air too poor to rob" tells us that the air is so polluted that not even smoke can make it any worse. This creates a feeling of tiredness, depression and uncleanliness. We feel that this man is a reject from society.

Morgan uses the sonnet form to emphasise his various images of decay and illness. We can see how, although the fourteen lines are presented in a single stanza, the first eight lines (octet) are in the form of two quatrains, each rhyming ABBA. The next six lines (sestet) are presented as two groups of three, each rhyming CDC.

The poet uses the first quatrain to explore the backcourt and surrounding area of the dilapidated and condemned tenement building, the next quatrain describes aspects of the building itself, the first three lines of the sestet take us into the last remaining occupied apartment and the final three lines focus on the lives of the occupants of this depressing place. It is as if the poet is steadily zooming in on his subject and the effect in the end is to emphasise very powerfully the impact that urban decay has on the lives of people.

Each of the first three lines of the sestet ends in a full stop so that we are invited to dwell for a moment on three aspects of the miserable interior of the apartment – the rats, the mould and the old cooker. By contrast the final three lines of the sestet run on into one another and this continuous flow helps to emphasise not just the sickly and aimless life of the man as he lies late in bed smoking cigarette after cigarette and coughing away but also the fact that his situation is ongoing and probably deteriorating.

Morgan also makes good use of the traditional sonnet rhyme scheme to emphasise some of the key images that he uses. A particularly good example of this is his rhyming of 'buttresses/mistresses'. The rhyme draws our attention to the irony of the descriptions – as if the tenement was a castle or a grand mansion and the poverty-stricken female occupants were ladies of the manor. The poet's rhyming of 'trash', ash', 'crash' smash' helps to emphasise the filth and perhaps also the violence associated with such a deprived setting.

Although the poem opens with the steady beat of a traditional iambic pentameter, Morgan is quick to change the metric pattern in order to point up certain words. In the second line, for example, the stress on the first syllable of 'hackles'/'puddles'/mattresses' helps to emphasise the miserable setting.

Later in the poem, the stress on 'Four storeys' and 'Roses of mould' helps to emphasise the extent of the vandalism of smashed windows and the irony that what we have inside the apartment is not beautiful flowers but rather rot and decay. Thus Morgan uses the traditional structure of the sonnet to draw our attention to these striking images

I believe that poverty alienates people in many ways. Morgan's poem and his powerful descriptions of the way in which urban decay impacts on the life of this one family confirmed and strengthened my understanding of the connection between the two (approx 1200 words)

Critical Essay (4)

What follows is a highly detailed analysis by the writer of this Guide of *'Assisi',* one of the six poems by Norman MacCaig that are included in the set Scottish texts section of the *Critical Reading* paper. You can develop similarly detailed analyses of the other five poems over time so that any extract that comes up will already have been fully studied. This sample detailed analysis is followed by sample answers to specimen questions on 'Sounds of the Day', another of MacCaig's poems.

Detailed analysis

Having been on a pilgrimage to Assisi myself, the title of the poem, Assisi, set up immediately in my mind associations with St Francis, the great saint of the Roman Catholic Church who came from there. I assumed that the poem might be about his life of piety, his humility and his love and caring for the very least of God's creatures and perhaps about the beauty of the great basilica built in honour of the saint. It is – but not in quite the way I expected.

The poet begins with a blunt description of a hideously deformed beggar who sits, alone and almost totally disregarded, outside the entrance to the great basilica in question.

In the second stanza, the poet takes us inside the basilica and comments on the explanations by a priest to a group of tourists about the beauty and the importance of a set of frescoes inside a chapel of the basilica that depict the life of St Francis as a true follower of the teachings of Christ.

In the third stanza the poet describes his impression of the tourist reactions to the priest's explanations before returning outside to the ugliness of the beggar's deformities and the fact that he remains largely disregarded.

The beggar is a man who attracts the love of no-one, it would seem, and least of all the shallow and hypocritical pilgrims and tourists who appear to be more impressed with the beauty of the basilica and its contents for themselves, rather than for their value as symbols of the love of God and His servant, St Francis. The poet uses simple yet powerful words and imagery to emphasise his point of view; likewise his use of free verse allows him to position key words within his poem in a way that strongly emphasises their importance to him.

MacCaig opens his poem with four run-on lines that convey with the clarity almost of a photograph the extent of the deformity of a beggar who sits at the door of the great basilica. The words 'dwarf' and 'hands on backwards' provide a quite shocking and gruesome introduction to his appearance, perhaps especially in a modern world where we try not to speak of people in such blunt terms. The images certainly clashed with the initial associations in my mind that were conveyed by the mere name, Assisi. And there is an irony in the suggestion that the basilica dwarfs the beggar instead of celebrating people like him as it was supposed to.

The alliteration of 'sat, slumped' and 'sack' and the deep sound of 'slumped' help to draw my attention not only to the physical appearance of the beggar but also to his

137

mood of dejection or despair. The simile, 'like a half-filled sack', the alliteration of 'tiny twisted legs' and the association of 'sawdust' all help to convey the impression of a scarecrow or imitation figure rather than a real human being. And perhaps, just as a burst bag of sawdust spills its contents over the ground so the man's life is ebbing away.

By placing the word 'outside' at the beginning of the next line, the poet succeeds in the remaining lines of the first stanza in emphasising the contrast between the magnificence of the basilica with its three tiers of churches and the sorry state of the man who should be a beneficiary of what it stands for – but isn't. It is almost as if the tiers of building form a kind of barrier, separating the ugliness outside from the beauty within.

The same word 'outside' and its placing simultaneously emphasises the impression that the man is a cast-off from society, an outsider and a reject who is neither loved nor wanted. There is very heavy irony on the word 'honour'. What is honourable about a building that is a symbol of great wealth and yet which keeps the poor and deformed at bay? And why spend so much on a memorial when it might have been better spent on the poor? No doubt, St Francis, as a 'brother of the poor' and 'a talker with birds' would have acknowledged the needs of the beggar but the modern world passes the man by and he might as well be dead, as surely he soon will be. The placing of the word 'yet' at the end of the first stanza rounds off the note of deep irony of the notion that the beggar's life could in anyway be described as an 'advantage' over anyone else's, let alone the life of St Francis.

In stanza two the poet takes us inside the church to where a priest is acting as a kind of tour guide and pointing out to a group of pilgrims the beauty and significance of a set of murals by the great Italian painter Giotto designed to celebrate the life of St Francis, and the goodness of God and the suffering of his Son which so inspired St Francis. It is not clear if the priest is leading the group of pilgrims who earlier had walked into the basilica with barely a glance at the beggar outside or whether he is a Franciscan who is helping to describe how the beauty of the murals inspires us to reflect on the goodness of God.

One way or another, the poet is quite caustic about the way in which the priest carries out his duties. The use of enjambment in this stanza helps to convey the impression of the priest rattling through a prepared script for the thousandth time. And the alliteration of 'goodness of God' and 'suffering Son' conveys the impression of an overused cliché rather than any great sincerity on the part of the priest.

No doubt, the murals were indeed originally inspired by and intended to convey the love of

God, his Son and St Francis. And no doubt, St Francis himself exemplified in his daily life his concern for the weak and the poor. The priest seems by contrast to be more of an intellectual or academic, more pleased perhaps to show off his intellectualism rather than his charity as Francis did.

There certainly is a clear note of criticism in these lines about the values that the priest seems to personify. The poet says that he understands and appreciates the points that the priest is making about the cleverness of the artist but there is the hint of a mocking suggestion that the priest is treating the tourists as being every bit as 'illiterate' as the poor uneducated country folk for whom the murals were originally designed.

There is, perhaps too, the suggestion of an unasked question that is emphasised by the poet's placing of the phrase 'the cleverness' on its own at the end of the stanza. If God is so good then why did He allow suffering at all? Why, for that matter, are deformed people created if God is so good? And as for the Church, perhaps it would have been cleverer to educate the poor to read and then the frescoes would not have been necessary.

The poet seems to be equally scathing in his attitudes towards the tourists, to whom he now turns at the start of the third stanza. The poet's scorn for them is conveyed in a complex mixture of metaphor, alliteration, onomatopoeia and allusion.

The pilgrims are like farmyard hens 'clucking contentedly' as they 'flutter' after the farmer who scatters grain to feed them. The alliteration emphasises the notion that the tourists are as happy to swallow the words of the priest as the farmyard fowl are to swallow grain. 'Flutter' not only reminds us of the sound of the beating wings of the hens or chickens as they dart this way and that in pursuit of the scattered grain, it also hints at the idea of the hearts of the pilgrims being all of a 'flutter' as they admire the words of the priest.

Again, however, there seems to be an even deeper meaning in these lines. 'The grain of the Word' is an obvious allusion to Christ's parable of the Sower and the Seed where Christ tells his disciples that spreading the word of God is rather like a farmer sowing seed – with some of it landing on good ground but some of it landing on stony ground. In drawing this comparison between Christ and the priest, the poet seems once again to be commenting on how far the 'cleverness' of the Church has become removed from Christ's original purposes.

At the same time, the poet is clearly implying that the tourists listening to the priest are perhaps personifying the 'stony ground' where the seeds, like the word of God, withered and died. The phrase, 'it was they' throws emphasis on to the word 'they'. They are the ones who walked past the beggar as they entered the basilica.

In the latter part of the second stanza the poet returns to where the beggar sits outside the basilica. He speaks of him as being 'a ruined temple'. This is a particularly powerful metaphor. There is an obvious contrast between the basilica and the 'temple' that is the body of the beggar. One represents wealth, the other poverty; one represents power, the other weakness. Then again, it would seem that the basilica represents superficiality and hypocrisy whereas the beggar represents inner beauty and real human spirit. Certainly, a clear contrast is made between the external ugliness of the beggar with his pus-filled eyes, humped back and twisted mouth and the inner beauty that is hinted at by the sweetness of his voice when he thanks those pilgrims who do take pity on him.

The poet's use of the word 'temple' made me wonder if he was alluding to the Christian idea that a person's body is a temple of the Holy Spirit and that therefore every single person has a unique dignity in the eyes of God. We are told that the eyes of the beggar 'wept pus'. Perhaps the poet is reminding us that Jesus too wept with compassion for the misfortune of others. Certainly, the concluding suggestion that the beggar's voice sounded as sweet as that of a child speaking to its mother or of the birds that spoke to St Francis suggests that the beggar might have more in common with the saint than the tourists have.

In these final lines, the poet is reminding us again and again that the beggar would have been treated with compassion by Christ or St Francis. The similes of 'like a child or bird' convey innocence and love but the careful placing of the name St Francis at the end of the poem emphasises and sums up the fact that these pilgrims, in their shallow indifference to the plight of the beggar are not in any way reflecting the standards of the saint or the God in whom they believe.

Overall, I enjoyed reading this poem very much. MacCaig writes about complex issues with great simplicity. I like how he often describes an autobiographical moment in his life to reflect upon some important aspect of the human condition. He also manages to convey a very great deal in a very succinct way. His imagery allows us to picture his people, places and points in our minds with great clarity. His use of free verse allows him to compose lines and to place words with great care so that he can maximise the impact of the points he is making. His use of contrast is particularly strong and he frequently succeeds in emphasising points by highlighting the differences between them.

Set text analysis

Note: The new CfE Higher English Critical Reading paper sees the introduction for the first time of a new type of question – set text analysis, with a range of extracts from the work of various Scottish authors being presented for your consideration. Do remember that you are required to analyse only *one* of the extracts in question. There are similarities between analysing literature and analysing the kind of prose passages that you have already encountered in the *UAE* Paper. Thus, for example, you may expect to be thinking again about word choice, imagery, structure, punctuation and tone and they ways in which these are used to emphasise points that the writer wishes to make.

The Specimen Higher English Critical Reading paper includes an extract from the work of Norman MacCaig, together with a range of questions. The extract (in this case a complete poem) and the specimen questions are presented below, together with sample answers to illustrate how this new type of question might be tackled.

Sounds of the Day: Norman MacCaig

When a clatter came,

it was horses crossing the ford.

When the air creaked, it was
a lapwing seeing us off the premises
of its private marsh. A snuffling puff
ten yards from the boat was the tide blocking
and unblocking a hole in a rock.
When the black drums rolled, it was water
falling sixty feet into itself.

When the door
scraped shut, it was the end
of all the sounds there are.

You left me
beside the quietest fire in the world.

I thought I was hurt in my pride only,
forgetting that,
when you plunge your hand in freezing water,
you feel
a bangle of ice round your wrist
before the whole hand goes numb.

Question 1: By referring closely to lines 1-9, analyse MacCaig's use of poetic technique to create a vivid sense of place.

Sample answer: In the first nine lines of the poem, the poet creates a vivid sense of place by focusing on what seem to be the typical sounds of his holiday life that are a source of recurring comfort and pleasure to him, before going on in each case to explain the sources of these sounds.

Thus the onomatopoeia of the word, 'clatter' seems to catch precisely the hard sound of horses hooves as they strike off the rocky bed of a local stream; similarly, the sharp, hard sound of the unusual word 'creaked' captures something of the noisy call of a lapwing warning trespassers away from its nest in the local marshes; the sound of waves gurgling in and out of crevices in the rocks when the poet is out in his boat is caught perfectly by the assonance of 'snuffling puff'; and finally the sound of a drum roll is compared to the sound of a local waterfall. For good measure, the poet's recurring use of the phrase 'when it was...' emphasises the recurring nature of these comforting sounds from his own little world, probably when he was on holiday on his beloved north-west coast of Scotland.

Question 2: By referring closely to lines 10-12, analyse MacCaig's use of poetic technique to convey the abrupt change in the poet's circumstances.

Sample answer: At first, the word 'When' makes us think momentarily that the poet is going to list another comforting sound. But this time, the alliteration and onomatopoeia of 'scraped shut' conveys the jarring screech of wood on floor as a tight-fitting door closes. There is the sound of pain here, not contentment. The image of a closed door itself suggests the closing of a stage in the poet's life. The end-placing of the word 'end' confirms the feeling of finality. The deliberate separation of these three lines from the rest emphasises the contrast between this new painful sound and the previous happy ones.

Question 3: By referring closely to lines 13-20 analyse how MacCaig highlights the impact which the parting has in the persona.

Sample answer: the persona seems bitter and numbed by what appears to be a terminal break-up in a relationship. The stress on each of the three words, 'You left me' and the very abruptness of the single line emphasises a tone of bitterness and a sense of rejection; the visual image of the 'quietest fire' contrasts sharply with the happy sounds of earlier times. The image of a hand being numbed by placing it in freezing water is particularly powerful. Just as there is at first only a 'bangle of ice' round the wrist before the whole hand goes numb, so the person will become completely numbed by the finality of this sad parting and the growing awareness of what has been lost.

Question 4: by referring to this poem and at least one other, discuss the poet's use of contrast to explore theme in his work.

Note:

Specimen marking instructions issued by the SQA for this new type of Critical Reading question indicate that candidates will score:

(a) 2 marks for identifying and summing up one overall permeating feature of the poet's work (such as his use of contrast)

(b) 2 marks for identifying, analysing and evaluating *one example* of the key feature in the *set extract* (over and above the analysis and evaluation of the extract that is called for in answering earlier questions)

(c) 2 marks *each* for identifying, analysing and evaluating a further *three examples* of the same feature in *one or more* other poems by MacCaig (Total: 10 marks)

Sample answer

(a) MacCaig was fond of using contrast in his poems because many of his poems explored the contradictions and changes in life and, by using contrast, he could highlight these contradictions and changes in the human condition. At the same time, his use of contrast helped to emphasise that the reality of human life is that we are all a mass of contradictions anyway and that we should be ready, as he is, to accept that simple fact.

(b) In 'Sounds of the Day', MacCaig, as we have seen, contrasts a series of pleasant familiar sounds with a jarring sound to emphasise the pain of a final, abrupt ending of a close relationship. The contrast between previous happiness and current pain is further emphasised when the poet describes the source of the harsh sound of a door that has 'scraped shut' *first* before describing the sound itself. In the case of all the other happier sounds, the sounds were described first and then their sources.

(c) In 'Assisi', MacCaig contrasts the appearance of a horribly deformed beggar with the beauty of a basilica and its fine frescoes. The 'cleverness' of the Church, as represented by one of its priests, is contrasted with its supposed mission of faith, hope and charity. And the indifference of pilgrims who pass by the beggar is also contrasted with the love and care that St Francis gave to such unfortunate people.

(i) In the early lines of 'Assisi', the use of the word 'dwarf' and phrases like 'hands on backwards' and the alliterative 'tiny twisted legs' emphasise the degree of deformity of the beggar who sits outside the basilica. All of this is contrasted with the 'three tiers' of the magnificent basilica itself, built ironically enough in honour of St Francis and his dedication to the poor and to society's outcasts. But now the basilica is being celebrated as a thing of beauty in its own right and the needs of the poor and the deformed are being disregarded.

(ii) In stanza two the poet is quite caustic about the way in which a priest carries out his duties. He contrasts the priest's 'cleverness' in explaining the significance of some frescoes with the true charity of St Francis and with the fact that there does not seem to be much evidence of the priest or anyone else practising what they or the frescoes preach. Again, the frescoes are being celebrated as art rather than as symbols of faith and love.

(iii) The poet is equally scathing in stanza three about the tourists listening to the priest. They are like farmyard hens 'clucking contentedly' as they 'flutter' after the farmer who scatters 'the grain of the Word' to feed them. 'This is an obvious allusion to Christ's parable of the Sower and the Seed where Christ tells his disciples that spreading the word of God is rather like a farmer sowing seed – with some of it landing on good ground but some of it landing on stony ground. In comparing the tourists to chickens, the poet is contrasting their selfish, witless concern for their own well-being with their total lack of concern for the unfortunate beggar or regard for his inner beauty. Clearly, these tourists represent the stony ground.

Critical Essay (5)
Specimen question: Choose a novel or short story in which a specific location or setting is crucial to the plot. Discuss how the writer makes you aware of the setting's importance and how the feature is used to enhance your appreciation of the text as a whole.

Sample answer
A short story in which the setting is crucial to the plot is 'The Pedestrian' by Ray Bradbury. The setting is a city of three million people, one hundred years in the future. The streets are empty of traffic, the pavements are in a state of disrepair and in the whole city only one person, Mr Leonard Mead, is out and about. That is the opening of the story. So what is going on? Has there been a nuclear war? The depressing answer unfolds as

Bradbury explores an issue that concerns him. As he describes the wanderings of his hero through the empty streets of the otherwise deserted city, it becomes clear that the issue in question is the growing impact that technology is having on our lives, particularly with regard to healthy pursuits.

Leonard Mead is the only human character in the story. And we do not learn all that much about him. He loves walking and goes out every night for a stroll. But he is the only person in a large city of three million who does so...The rest have all long since given up walking and spend their leisure time at home in front of TVs.

One night while out walking, Leonard is stopped by a remote-controlled police car, the only kind of police presence that is required in a city where there is no longer any crime as no one goes out any more.

The police car interrogates Leonard about what he is up to. It finds it difficult to believe that he is simply out for a walk. Nobody in his right mind goes out for a walk. Leonard is arrested and taken away to the centre for regressive tendencies. So now there is no one left who goes out walking. The city lies completely empty.

The story is a fine example of the skills that placed Bradbury among the greatest of science fiction writers. He takes a look at some aspect of current human behaviour that concerns him and then projects forward a hundred years or so to explore what might happen in future if the aspect of human behaviour is not changed. Thus his stories provide a warning for us about undesirable aspects of human behaviour in order to get us to change our ways before it is too late.

Bradbury also has a poetic style of writing that captures our interest and helps us to envisage the people and the places that he is describing almost as if they are being filmed. In this case, the city itself is the focus of his attention.

Bradbury captures our attention straight away. He speaks of 'the silence that was the city at eight o'clock of a misty evening'. And he talks of 'the buckling concrete walk' and 'the grassy seams'. What kind of city is silent at that time of night? What kind of city is in such a state of disrepair? The answer is a city where no one goes out walking any more, a city where a pedestrian like his hero, Mr Leonard Mead is 'alone, or as good as alone'. His name has a gentle, old world sound,

Bradbury's descriptions of the long avenues along which Leonard strolls each night are particularly poetic. Passing by darkened houses is like 'walking through a graveyard' where 'grey phantoms' whisper and murmur at the windows of 'tomb-like' buildings. Leonard has even taken to wearing soft shoes so that he won't set off dogs to barking as he strolls along. The city feels eerie and empty.

Bradbury uses very strong imagery to convey the sense of the isolation of Mr Mead in the apparently deserted city. As he walks, his moving shadow is 'like the shadow of a hawk in mid-country'. If he closes his eyes, it is easy for him to imagine himself in the middle of a 'wintry, windless Arizona desert'. The city streets are 'like dry river beds'. In ten years of walking thousands of miles, he has never met another person walking. City streets may be busy during the day with a 'thunderous surge' of cars as people go about their daily business. But at night the city highways are 'like streams in a dry season'. This series of similes provides us with a clear impression of the lonely nature of Leonard's walks. We also get the impression that he is isolated from his fellow man. There is little in the way of social intercourse.

Everyone else, it seems, is sitting at home, transfixed by the banality of television programmes. Mr Mead shares his thoughts with us by thinking out loud about the rather trivial programmes that the rest of the city population are watching. Westerns, assorted murder mysteries and 'a comedian falling off a stage' seem to be the norm. As far as he is concerned, people who sit endlessly at home watching such programmes are 'like the dead in their tombs', the light of the television touching their faces 'but never really touching them'. They learn nothing, it seems. They are like zombies.

Leonard turns back for home and is almost there when he is stopped by a lone police car. 'The light held him fixed, like a museum specimen'. This fine simile emphasises the control of the machine over him. As the last person around who enjoys walking, he is indeed a museum specimen. Leonard is interrogated with a series of rapid-fire questions about who he is and why he is out walking. 'What are you doing out? Walking? Walking where? For what?'

The police car, which turns out to be a remotely controlled vehicle, can make no sense of his answers. When he describes himself as a writer, the car records that as no profession. Why should he be out 'walking for air and walking to see' when he has air conditioning at home and a television? The machine cannot understand the man. The sequence of questions highlights the puzzlement of the police. Eventually, he is told to get into the car so that he can be taken to the 'Centre for Regressive Tendencies'. The inside of the car smells of 'riveted steel'. There is nothing of soft humanity about it.

On the way, the car passes by Leonard's home, the only house that is lit up, the last beacon of hope in an otherwise dark world. Leonard's house, like Leonard himself is the last symbol of a way of life that is dying. And so we are left with the 'empty streets with the empty sidewalks and no sound and no motion'. The repetition has a note of finality about it. From now on, it seems, there will be no one left to enjoy the simple pleasures of a stroll. Leonard is our last representative and now he has gone, Technology has won and mankind has ceased to exist, as it were. Only the deserted city, it seems, remains.

Thus we can see that in this short story the setting, rather than, for example, character has the greatest impact on us so far as the moral of the story is concerned. (approx 1200 words)

Critical Essay (6)
Specimen question: Choose a work of biography or autobiography in which the writer's description of an emotional experience creates a powerful impression. Briefly explain the emotional experience and then discuss how the writer's description of this experience creates this powerful impression.

Analysis of question:
In this final specimen question, we see clearly again the typical pattern of such questions: the invitation to identify a text that is *relevant* to the terms of the question; the invitation briefly to *demonstrate understanding* of the essential content and 'message' of the text; the invitation to *analyse* the techniques or features used by the writer to put that message over; and the invitation to *evaluate*

the text in terms of its overall impact on you, the reader.

Sample answer

George Orwell's autobiographical essay, 'A Hanging' describes an emotional experience that creates a powerful impression. He attacks capital punishment in this essay by sharing with us the way he felt when, as a superintendent of police in Burma in the early 1920s, he had to attend a hanging.

He does not get into an academic debate about the pros and cons of hanging. Nor does he even tell us what the condemned man did or whether or not he deserved the death sentence. But he focuses very powerfully on the mood of the occasion and describes it with such clarity and emotion that we are drawn to sympathise with his point of view.

Orwell establishes a dark mood from the very outset. It is a 'sodden morning of rains'. Nature itself seems to be in mourning. The sun offers only 'a sickly light, like yellow tinfoil', a vivid image of illness and disease. The condemned cells are 'like small animal cages' and the use of transferred epithet and simile emphasises the fate of the prisoners and the way they are treated.

Orwell now focuses on the prisoner who is to be hanged. He is a 'puny wisp' of a man who seems almost like a comic figure with his absurdly big moustache. Yet he is surrounded by six tall Indian warders and is threatened with rifles and bayonets while he is handcuffed and chained as if he is a dangerous maniac who cold strike out and kill at any moment. In fact, the prisoner is passive and yielding and the description of his harsh handling makes us more inclined to sympathise with his plight.

The superintendent of the prison is uncaring, however. Ironically enough he is an army doctor but his only concern is to get the hanging over and done with so that everyone can have their breakfast.

The ceremony is suddenly interrupted by the appearance of a large dog that prances about barking with glee at seeing so many people and dodging every effort to capture it. Just for good measure, it starts licking the face of the prisoner. He is, after all, just another human being as far as the dog is concerned.

At first there is almost a sense of shock and everyone stands aghast at this breech of protocol before the dog is finally captured and led away. Meanwhile, the lively curiosity of the dog is contrasted with the indifference of the prisoner. It is almost as if prancing dogs are part of the formalities, as far as he is concerned.

Orwell then describes in detail every movement of the prisoner as he moves towards the gallows. 'The lock of his hair danced up and down, his feet printed themselves on the wet gravel.' He even steps aside to avoid a puddle. These simple details emphasise how alive and well the man is. Yet he is soon to be put to death. It is at this point that Orwell expresses directly his opposition to 'the unspeakable wrongness of cutting a life short when it is in full tide.' The condemned man was a fully functioning unique human being and yet he would be gone 'with a sudden snap – one mind less, one world less'. To Orwell, every single human life is important.

Orwell then goes on to describe the details of the gallows and the details of the hanging procedure in simple, factual but powerful language. Once the prisoner is in position, he begins to chant repetitively, Ram! Ram! Ram! The onlookers begin to feel the strain – everyone had changed colour – and Orwell admits that, like the others, he wished the hanging was over just to stop 'that abominable noise!' Suddenly there is 'a clanking noise and then dead silence'. The man is 'as dead as a stone'. The use of onomatopoeia, pun and simile emphasise the sudden finality of it all.

Orwell then admits that he shares with the others 'enormous relief' now that the event is over. There is a kind of hysteria with everyone laughing and giggling and chatting, as if to avoid thinking about what they have done. Everyone, including Orwell, roars with laughter as the head jailer describes the problems that a previously condemned man gave his captors by wriggling about at the end of the rope and requiring the doctor to pull on his legs to ensure death.

The use of direct speech as the jailer tells his tale even has the reader smiling. 'My dear fellow', we said, 'think of all the pain and trouble you are causing us!' Meanwhile, the irony of the doctor's interpretation of his prime purpose to do no harm is obvious. Everyone ends up having a friendly drink, with the dead man already forgotten a hundred yards away.

Orwell succeeds, as a result of his very precise descriptions, in providing us with a graphic picture of this very emotional experience and of the various reactions to it. He is ashamed to admit that in many ways he simply reacted in the same way as the others. But this sincerity helps to emphasise the strength of his belief that capital punishment is wrong.

It is easy to imagine that in his day, Orwell's essay would have been the subject of much debate about capital punishment. By focusing on the fate of one apparently insignificant man, he emphasises the fundamental wrongness of taking a life. Through the clarity of his descriptions and his sincere expressions of his emotions, Orwell certainly succeeded in convincing me that capital punishment is an 'unspeakable wrongness'. (Approx 900 words)

In conclusion

These samples of critical essay answers all follow a reasonably simple structure:

• An opening sentence where you turn the words of the question into a statement to ensure that the answer which follows is relevant

• A brief paragraph where you demonstrate your understanding of what the text is essentially about

• A series of paragraphs that summarise textual contents *relevant to the question being asked* and analyse the features used by the writer to put the 'message' over

• A series of sentences where your points are followed by examples of your points in the shape of close reference to, and even quotes from, the text.

• Sentences which focus on the impact on you, the reader, of the various techniques that the writer is using

• A conclusion that sums up the way in which you have answered the question by going back for a final time to the words of the question

Above all, *immerse* yourself in your favourite works of literature but then focus in your answers only on those features that are relevant to the questions you are asked. *Carpe diem*!

Selected sources of further advice

Type, or copy and paste if working with an e-book, the following URLS into your browser and you will have free access to a range of advice, examples, answers and comments on all parts of the CfE Higher English paper. The materials are either indispensable or merely excellent.

NB: Web sites and URLS can change over time so if you have problems enter phrases into Google such as *marking instructions Higher English folio* or *Higher English critical reading* or *Higher English Specimen Paper* and so on and you will find the materials. Or simply search www.sqa.org.uk

Writing Portfolio
http://www.sqa.org.uk/files_ccc/CfE_Cours eSpecification_Higher_Languages_English .pdf - details about the course specification for CfE Higher English after August, 2014

   http://www.sqa.org.uk/files_ccc/Candida teGuideEnglishWritingFolioHigher.pdf - example of, and links to, essential candidate guides from the *Scottish Qualification Authority (SQA)* about the *portfolio, reading for understanding, analysis and evaluation* and *critical reading*

   http://www.sqa.org.uk/files_ccc/WritingF olio-HigherMIS.pdf - criteria, category descriptors and marking instructions for the Higher English writing portfolio that describe clearly to markers (and therefore to candidates) what is looked for

www.bbc.co.uk/bitesize/higher/english - excellent source of revision tips for all sections of the CfE Higher English exam

http://mycourse.solent.ac.uk/mod/book/tool/print/index.php?id=2732#ch1104 – very useful guide to personal reflective writing

http://www.wikihow.com/Write-a-Persuasive-Essay - useful advice and examples of persuasive essays

Understanding, Analysis and Evaluation
www.sqa.org.uk/pastpapers - indispensable source of recent past papers and Specimen Papers in the new format CfE Higher English exam, together with marking instructions and other key information. Older papers (e.g. Higher English, 2004) can be searched for online, using Google or any other search engine

http://www.sqa.org.uk/files/nq/c03912_sqp.pdf - specimen marking instructions for the *UAE* paper

http://www.sqa.org.uk/sqa/files_ccc/SQPH_English_SQP_2011.pdf - specimen *UAE* and *Critical Essay* papers adapted from a past paper with detailed marking instructions

http://www.sqa.org.uk/files_ccc/Higher%20English%20Close%20Reading%20Final%20Q.pdf – detailed explanation of how to answer and mark the comparison question in the *UAE* paper

Seely, John (2013) *An A-Z of Grammar and Punctuation, Oxford* - all you need to know, and more about the joys of English grammar

Critical Reading
http://www.sqa.org.uk/pastpapers/papers/instructions/2012/mi H English Critical-Essay 2012.pdf - example of the kind of information and instructions that are issued each year to markers of critical essays and which provide an excellent indication to candidates as the kind of standard that is looked for in such essays

www.cliffsnotes.com; www.sparknotes.com; www.shmoop.com – excellent study guides to help your understanding of favourite poetry, drama and prose

http://www.bbc.co.uk/education/guides/zcr6fg8/revision a detailed discussion of MacCaig's poetry, focusing on the poems that are listed for CfE Higher English

http://www.sqa.org.uk/sqa/files ccc/SQP H English SQP 2011.pdf - specimen *UAE paper and Critical Essay* paper with detailed marking instructions (also listed in the *UAE* section above

http://www.sqa.org.uk/files ccc/English SQPHPPGuidance.pdf - Guidance on using past paper questions relevant to the new format

Lightning Source UK Ltd.
Milton Keynes UK
UKHW010643240519
343267UK00001B/382/P

9 781785 070655